# ECHOGRAPHIES OF
# TELEVISION

# ECHOGRAPHIES OF
# TELEVISION

## FILMED INTERVIEWS

JACQUES DERRIDA AND
BERNARD STIEGLER

Translated by Jennifer Bajorek

polity

Copyright this translation Polity Press 2002. First published in France as *Échographies de la télévision. Entretiens filmés*, © Éditions Galilée, 1996.

First published in 2002 by Polity Press in association with Blackwell Publishers Ltd, a Blackwell Publishing Company

Published with the assistance of the French Ministry of Culture.

*Editorial office*:
Polity Press
65 Bridge Street
Cambridge CB2 1UR, UK

*Marketing and production*:
Blackwell Publishers Ltd
108 Cowley Road
Oxford OX4 1JF, UK

*Published in the USA by*
Blackwell Publishers Inc.
350 Main Street
Malden, MA 02148, USA

ISBN 0–7456–2036–1
ISBN 0–7456–2037–X (pbk)

A catalogue record for this book is available from the British Library and has been applied for from the Library of Congress.

Typeset in 11 on 13 pt Sabon
by Graphicraft Limited, Hong Kong
Printed in Great Britain by TJ International Ltd, Padstow, Cornwall

This book is printed on acid-free paper.

# CONTENTS

List of Illustrations                                              vi
Translator's Note                                                viii


## Artifactualities
### Jacques Derrida                                                1


## Echographies of Television
### Jacques Derrida and Bernard Stiegler                          29

1  Right of Inspection                                             31
2  Artifactuality, Homohegemony                                    41
3  Acts of Memory: Topolitics and Teletechnology                  56
4  Inheritances – and Rhythm                                       68
5  The "Cultural Exception": The States of the State,
   the Event                                                       73
6  The Archive Market: Truth, Testimony, Evidence                  82
7  Phonographies: Meaning – from Heritage to Horizon              100
8  Spectrographies                                                113
9  Vigilances of the Unconscious                                  135


## The Discrete Image
### Bernard Stiegler                                              145


Notes                                                             164

# ILLUSTRATIONS

Jacques Derrida, INA (Institut National de l'Audiovisuel),
"Voluntary Memory," interview, Jacques Derrida with
Bernard Stiegler, December 1993 (photo Michel Lioret,
© INA)     32

Bernard Stiegler, INA, "Voluntary Memory," interview,
Jacques Derrida with Bernard Stiegler, December 1993
(photo Michel Lioret, © INA)     61

"Gulf War News," frame from an audiovisual reading
station (photo Nicole Bouron, © INA)     78

"Rodney King Beating," Los Angeles, March 1991
(© Frank Spooner Pictures/Liaison)     91

"Portrait of Lewis Payne," Alexander Gardner, 1865
(Library of Congress)     114

Roland Barthes, 1975, "The Lefty" (photo Daniel
Boudinet, © Ministry of Culture, France)     116

Exchange between Pascale Ogier and Jacques Derrida,
frame from *Ghostdance*, dir. Ken McMullen, Loose Yard
LTD, Channel Four, ZDF, 1983 (all rights reserved)     118

Jacques Derrida, INA, "Voluntary Memory," interview,
Jacques Derrida with Bernard Stiegler, December 1993
(photo Michel Lioret, © INA)     119

Pascale Ogier, frame from *Ghostdance*, dir. Ken
McMullen, Loose Yard LTD, Channel Four, ZDF, 1983
(all rights reserved)    121

Jacques Derrida, INA, "Voluntary Memory," interview,
Jacques Derrida with Bernard Stiegler (photo Michel
Lioret, © INA)    138

# TRANSLATOR'S NOTE

In "Artifactualities," points of ellipsis in square brackets reproduce those appearing in the edition published by Galilée and the Institut National de l'Audiovisuel and indicate cuts made to the text of the interview for that edition. When not in brackets, the three points indicate Derrida's and Stiegler's own ellipses or suspensions, passim. I have also placed in brackets my interpolations in the text and in the authors' notes.

I have tried, where possible, to err on the side of the conversational (inserting French words and phrases only to bring out a pun or an etymological relation; keeping my notes to a minimum). Whether the fact that the bulk of the conversation transcribed in this volume was filmed or "televised" will have magnified or in some other way marked the impossibility of the translator's task is, in a sense, its very topic.

I am indebted to Dawn Anderson, Julia Lupton, and Michael Naas for their help with sources, to Ann Bone for her careful copy-editing, to Tom Keenan for his correction of a particularly egregious footnote, to Gene Kopan for workspace, and to Stuart Naifeh for his fearless first reading of the manuscript. I owe special thanks to Sam Weber for recommending me for this project at a particularly opportune moment. For their patient responses to my questions, I am grateful to Bernard Stiegler and, especially, to Jacques Derrida.

# ARTIFACTUALITIES

*Jacques Derrida*

Excerpts from an interview with Jacques Derrida conducted by Stéphane Douailler, Émile Malet, Cristina de Peretti, Brigitte Sohm, and Patrice Vermeren and published in *Passages*, no. 57 (Sept. 1993).

[ . . . ] Today, more than ever before, to think one's time, especially when one takes the risk or chance of speaking publicly about it, is to register, in order to bring it into play, the fact that the time of this very speaking is artificially produced. It is an *artifact*. In its very happening, the time of this public gesture is calculated, constrained, "formatted," "initialized" by a media apparatus (let's use these words so that we can move quickly). This would deserve nearly infinite analysis. Who today would think his time and who, above all, would speak about it, I'd like to know, without first paying some attention to a public space[1] and therefore to a political present which is constantly transformed, in its structure and its content, by the teletechnology of what is so confusedly called information or communication?

[ . . . ] Schematically, *two traits* [ . . . ] distinguish what makes [*ce qui fait*] actuality in general.[2] We might give them two portmanteau nicknames: *artifactuality* and *actuvirtuality*. The first trait is that actuality is, precisely, *made* [faite]:[3] in order to know what it's made of, one needs nonetheless to know that it is made. It is not given but actively produced, sifted, invested, performatively interpreted by numerous apparatuses which are *factitious* or *artificial*, hierarchizing and selective, always in the service of forces and interests to which "subjects" and agents (producers and consumers of actuality – sometimes they are "philosophers" and always interpreters, too) are never sensitive enough. No matter how singular, irreducible, stubborn, distressing or tragic the "reality" to which it refers, "actuality" comes to us by way of a fictional fashioning. It can be analyzed only at the cost of a labor

3

of resistance, of vigilant counter-interpretation, etc. Hegel was right to remind the philosopher of his time to read the papers daily. Today, the same responsibility obliges him to learn how the dailies, the weeklies, the television news programs are *made*, and *by whom*. He must ask to see things from the other side, from the side of the press agencies as well as from that of the teleprompter. We ought never to forget the full import of this index: when a journalist or politician seems to be speaking to us, in our homes, while looking us straight in the eye, he (or she) is in the process of reading, on screen, at the dictation of a "prompter," a text composed somewhere else, at some other time, sometimes by others, or even by a whole network of anonymous authors.

[. . .] We must develop a critical culture, a kind of education, but I would never say "we must" or "he must" or "it is necessary" [*"il faudrait"*], I would never speak of the citizen's any more than the philosopher's duty without adding two or three preliminary cautions.

The first concerns the question of the *national*. [. . .] Among the filterings that "inform" actuality, and despite an accelerated but all the more equivocal internationalization, there is this ineradicable privilege of the national, the regional, the provincial – or the Western – which overdetermines all the other hierarchies (first sports, then the "politician" – and not the political – then the "cultural," in supposedly decreasing order of demand, spectacularity, and legibility). This privilege relegates to a secondary position a whole host of events: those thought to be too far removed from the nation's (supposedly public) interest, from its vicinity, from the national language, code, and style. In the news, "actuality" is spontaneously ethnocentric. It excludes the foreigner, at times inside the country, quite apart from any nationalist passion, doctrine, or declaration, and even when this news [*ces "actualités"*] speaks of "human rights." Some journalists make laudable efforts to escape this law, but, by definition, it can't be done enough, and in the final analysis it is not up to the professional journalists. We mustn't forget this, especially today, when old nationalisms are taking on unprecedented forms by exploiting the most "advanced" media techniques (the official radio and television networks of ex-Yugoslavia would only be a particularly striking example). Let me say in passing that, not too long ago, some people felt compelled to call the critique of ethnocentrism into question, or, simplifying its image a great deal, the deconstruction of Eurocentrism. There are places where this is still acceptable today, as if these people remained blind to everything that is bringing death in the name of the ethnos, in the heart of Europe itself, in a Europe whose only reality, whose only "actuality," today is economic and national, and whose only law, in the case of alliances as well as conflicts, remains that of the market.

But the tragedy stems, as always, from a contradiction or double postulate: the apparent internationalization of the sources of information is often based on an appropriation and concentration of information and broadcast capital. Remember what happened during the Gulf War. That this represented an exemplary moment of awakening, and, here and there, rebellion, should not conceal the generality and invariability of this violence, in every conflict, in the Middle East and in other places. Sometimes, a "national" resistance to this apparently international homogenization may therefore also make itself felt. This is the first complication.

Another caution: this international artifactuality, this mono-polization of the "actuality effect," this centralizing appropriation of artifactual powers for "creating the event," may be accompanied by advances in the domain of "live" communication, or communication in so-called real time, in the present (tense). The theatrical genre of the "interview" sacrifices, at least in fiction, at the altar of this idolatry of "immediate," live presence. A newspaper always prefers to publish an interview with a photographed author – rather than an article that takes responsibility for reading, for evaluation, for pedagogy. And so, how to proceed without denying ourselves these new resources of live television (the videocamera, etc.) while continuing to be critical of their mystifications? And above all, while continuing to remind people and to *demonstrate* that the "live" and "real time" are never pure, that they do not give us intuition or transparency, a perception stripped of interpreta-tion or technical intervention. Any such demonstration already appeals, in and of itself, to philosophy.

Finally, as I suggested too quickly a moment ago, the requisite deconstruction of this *artifactuality* should not be used as an alibi. It should not give way to an inflation [*une surenchère*] of the simulacrum and neutralize every threat in what might be called the delusion of the delusion, the denial of the event: "Everything," people would then think, "even violence, suffering, war, and death, everything is constructed, fictionalized, constituted by and for the media apparatus. Nothing ever really happens. There is nothing but simulacrum and delusion." While taking the deconstruction of artifactuality as far as possible, we must therefore do everything in our power to guard against this critical neoidealism and remember, not only that a consistent deconstruction is a thinking of singularity, and therefore of the event, of what it ultimately preserves of the irreducible, but also that "information" is a contradictory and heterogeneous process. It can and must be transformed, it can and it must serve, as it has often done, knowledge, truth, and the cause of democracy to come, and all the questions they necessarily entail. We can't help but hope that artifactuality, as artificial and manipulative as it may be, will surrender[4] or yield to the coming of what comes, to the event that bears it and toward which it is borne. And to which it will bear witness, even if only despite itself.

[. . .] If we had the time, I would insist on another trait of "actuality," of what is happening today and of what is happening, today, *to actuality*. I would insist not only on the *artificial* synthesis (synthetic image, synthetic voice, all the prosthetic supplements that can take the place of real actuality), but above all on a concept of *virtuality* (virtual image, virtual space, and so virtual event) that can doubtless no longer be opposed, in perfect philosophical serenity, to actual [*actuelle*] reality in the way that philosophers used to distinguish between power and act, *dynamis* and *energeia*, the potentiality of a material and the defining form of a *telos*, and therefore also of a *progress*, etc. This virtuality makes its mark even on the structure of the produced event. It affects both the time and the space of the image, of discourse, of "information," in short, everything that refers us to this so-called actuality, to the implacable reality of its supposed present. Today, a philosopher who "thinks his time" must, among other things, be attentive to the implications and consequences of this virtual time. To the innovations in its technical implementation, but also to what the new recalls of much more ancient possibilities.

[. . .] The least acceptable thing on television, on the radio, or in the newspapers today is for intellectuals to take their time or to waste other people's time there. Perhaps this is what must be changed in actuality: its rhythm. Media professionals aren't supposed to waste any time. Neither theirs nor ours. Which they are nonetheless often sure to do. They know the cost, if not the value, of time. Before denouncing, as is constantly done, the silence of the intellectuals, why not give some thought to this new mediatic situation? And to the effects of a difference in rhythm? It can reduce certain intellectuals to silence (those who require a bit more time for the necessary analyses, and who refuse to adapt the complexity of things to the conditions imposed on their discussion); it can shut them up or drown out their voices with the sound of others – at least in places where certain rhythms and certain forms of speech are dominant. This other time, media time, gives rise above all to another distribution, to other spaces, rhythms, relays, forms of speaking out and public intervention. What is invisible, illegible, inaudible on the largest screen can be active and effective, immediately or in the long run, and disappears only in the eyes of those who confuse actuality with what they see or think they are doing in the window of a superstore.[5] In any case, this transformation of public space calls for work, and the work is being done, I think, it is more or less understood in all the places you'd expect. The silence of those who read the papers, listen to or watch the radio and television news programs, and who analyze them, is not really as silent as it seems in those places where precisely these papers and programs seem or become deaf – or deafen – to everything that does not speak according to their law. Hence we ought to turn the proposition around: a certain noise that the media make about a pseudo-actuality falls like silence, it keeps quiet about everything that speaks and acts. And that can be heard elsewhere or from another quarter, if one knows how to listen. This is the law of time; it is terrible for the present; it always leaves us hoping, leaving us to reckon with the untimely. It would be necessary to speak, here, of the effective limits of the right of response[6] (and therefore of democracy): they stem, quite apart from any deliberate censorship, from the appropriation of time and of public space, from their technical adjustment by those who exercise media power.

If I nonetheless allow myself this pause or this pose, a way like any other – for they are ways, yes – of thinking one's time, it is only because I am actually trying, in every way possible, to answer: to answer your questions by holding myself answerable or responsible for an interview. In order to assume this responsibility, one has got at least to know for what and for whom an interview is intended, particularly when it is with someone who also writes books, teaches, or publishes elsewhere, at another rhythm, in other situations, calculating his phrases otherwise. An interview should provide a snapshot, a movie still, a freeze frame: This is how this person, on this day, in this place, with these interlocutors, struggles like an animal in a difficult position. For example, when someone speaks to him of actuality, of what happens in the world every day, and if someone asks him to say in two words what he thinks about it, he suddenly retreats into his lair, like a hunted beast, he engages in endless chicanery, he drags you into a maze of cautions, delays and relays, he repeats in a thousand different ways: "Wait, it's not that simple" (which always agitates or elicits a snicker from those fools for whom things are always simpler than you think). Or again: "Sometimes one complicates in order to avoid, but simplification is an even more reliable strategy of avoidance." And so you have a virtual photograph: when faced with a question like yours, this is the gesture I'm most likely to make. It is neither purely impulsive nor entirely calculated. It consists, not in refusing to answer a question or somebody, but rather in trying to respect circumstantial conditions or invisible detours as much as possible.

[. . .] A philosopher may be concerned with the present, with what presently presents itself, with what is happening today [*actuellement*], without asking himself bottomless questions about what this value of presence signifies, presupposes, or hides. Will he be a philosopher of the present? Yes – but no. Another may do just the opposite: he may be immersed in a meditation about presence or about the presentation of the present without paying the slightest bit of attention to what is presently happening in the world or around him. Will he be a philosopher of the present? No – but yes. And yet, I am sure that no philosopher-worthy-of-the-name would accept this opposition. Like anyone trying to be a philosopher, I want very much not to give up either on the present or on thinking the presence of the present – nor on the experience of that which, even as it gives them to us, conceals them. For example, in what we were just calling artifactuality. How best to approach this theme of presence and of the present? On what conditions does one investigate this subject? What do these questions commit or put at stake? This commitment, this stake – isn't it essentially the law that would command everything, directly or indirectly? I am trying to observe it. By definition, this law remains inaccessible, beyond everything.

[. . .] What does this mean, to speak of the present? Of course, it would be easy to show that I have in fact never been concerned with anything but problems of actuality, with problems of institutional politics or of politics, period. And I could cite many examples, references, names, dates, places, etc. But I don't want to take the mediagogical easy way out and take advantage of this debate to indulge in some kind of self-justification. [. . .]

But I'm also trying not to forget that it is often untimely approaches to what is called actuality that are the most "concerned" with the present. In other words, to be concerned with the present, as a philosopher for example, may be to avoid constantly confusing the present with actuality. There is an anachronistic way of treating actuality which does not necessarily miss what is most present today. The difficulty, risk, or chance, the incalculable element, perhaps, would take the form of an untimeliness that comes in time: this one and not another, this one that comes *just in time*, *just* because it is anachronistic and disadjusted (like justice, which is always without measure, foreign to justness[7] or the norm of adaptation, heterogeneous to the very law it is supposed to command), more present than the present of actuality, more attuned to the singular excess [*démesure*] that marks the violent entrance of the other in the course of history. This entrance always takes an untimely, prophetic, or messianic form, and yet it needs no clamor or spectacle. It can remain almost inapparent. For the reasons we just mentioned, it is not in the daily papers that people are doing the most talking about this plupresent [*plusque-présent*] of today. Which is not to say that this is happening every day in the weeklies or monthlies either.

[. . .] A responsible response to the urgency of actuality calls for these cautions. It calls for dissent, for the dissonance and discord of this untimeliness, the just disadjustment of this anachrony. One must at one and the same time defer, distance oneself, hang back, *and* rush into things headlong. One must respond in such a way that one comes as close as possible to what comes to pass through actuality. At one and the same time each time, and each time it is another time, the first and the last. In any case, I like gestures (they are so rare, probably even impossible, and in any case, nonprogrammable) which unite the hyperactual with the anachronistic. And the preference for this union or admixture of styles is never simply a matter of taste. It is the law of response or of responsibility, the law of the other.

[. . .] Perhaps this brings us back to a more philosophical order of the response, the one we started with when we spoke of the thematics of the present or of presence, which is also to say, of the theme of différance, which has often been accused of privileging delay, neutralization, suspension and, consequently, of straying too far from the urgency of the present, particularly its ethical or political urgency. I have never understood there to be an opposition between urgency and différance. Dare I say, *on the contrary?* Again, this would be to simplify things too much. "At the same time" that it marks a *rapport* (a *ference*[8]) – a relation to what is other, to what differs in the sense of alterity, and therefore to alterity, to the singularity of the other – différance also relates, and for this very reason, to what comes, to what happens in a way that is at one and the same time inappropriable, unexpected, and therefore urgent, unanticipatable: precipitation itself. The thinking of différance is therefore also a thinking of urgency, of what I can neither evade nor appropriate because it is other. The event, the singularity of the event, that's what différance is all about. (This is why I said that it signifies something completely different from this neutralization of the event on the pretext that it has been artifactualized by the media.) Even if it also contains within itself, inevitably, "at the same time" (this "at one and the same time" [*"à la fois"*], this "same time" [*"même temps"*] whose same is going out of tune with itself all the time, an *out of joint* [in English in the original] time, a deranged, dislocated, off its hinges, disproportionate time, as Hamlet says), a countermovement that would reappropriate, divert, slacken, that would amortize the cruelty of the event and quite simply death [*la mort*], to which it surrenders.[9] Thus différance is a thinking that tries to surrender to the imminence of what is coming or going to come, of the event, and so to experience itself, insofar as experience tends just as inevitably, "at the same time," with a view to the "same time," to appropriate what happens: economy and aneconomy of the other at once. There would be no différance without urgency, imminence, precipitation, the ineluctable, the unforeseeable coming of the other, to whom both reference and deference are made.

[. . .] The event is another name for that which, in the thing that happens, we can neither reduce nor deny (or simply deny). It is another name for experience itself, which is always experience of the other. The event cannot be subsumed under any other concept, not even that of being. The "there is" ["*il y a*"] or the "that there is something rather than nothing" belongs, perhaps, to the experience of the event rather than to a thinking of being. The coming of the event is what we cannot and must never prevent, another name for the future itself. Not that it is good, good in and of itself, that everything or anything might happen. Not that we should give up trying to prevent certain things from happening (for then there would be no decision, no responsibility, ethical, political, or other). But we are only ever opposed to those events that we think obstruct the future or bring death, to those events that put an end to the possibility of the event, to the affirmative opening for the coming of the other. This is why a thinking of the event always opens a certain messianic space – as abstract, formal, and barren, as un-"religious" as it must be – and why this messianic dimension cannot be separated from justice, which here again I distinguish from law or right (as I have proposed to do in "Force of Law" and in *Specters of Marx*,[10] of which this is essentially the basic claim). If the event is what comes, occurs, arises [*vient, advient, survient*], it is not enough to say that this *coming* "is" not, that it cannot be reduced to some category of being. Nor do the noun ("coming" [*la venue*]) or the nominalized verb ("coming" [*le venir*]) exhaust the "come" [*"viens"*] from which they come.[11] I have often tried, elsewhere, to analyze this kind of performative apostrophe, this call that does not conform to the being of anything that is. Addressed to the other, it doesn't yet simply speak or say the desire, the command, the prayer, the demand that it surely announces and may subsequently make possible. The event must be thought on the basis of this "come" and not the other way around. "Come" is said to the other, to others that have yet to be determined as persons, subjects, equals (at least not in the sense of an equality that would be calculable). It is on condition of this "come" that there is an experience of coming, of the event, of what is happening, and consequently, of that which, because it comes from the other, cannot be anticipated. There is not even a horizon of expectation for this messianicity before messianism. If there were a horizon of expectation, if there were anticipation or programming, there would be neither event nor history. (A hypothesis which, paradoxically, and for the same reasons, can never be rationally excluded: it is practically impossible to think the absence of a horizon of expectation.) In order for there to be event and history, there must be a "come" that opens and addresses itself to someone, to someone else that I cannot and must not determine in advance, not as subject, self, consciousness, nor even as animal, god, or person, man or woman, living or non-living thing. (It must be possible to *summon* [appeler] a specter, to appeal to it [*en appeler à lui*], for example, and this is not just one example among others: perhaps there is something of the ghost [*revenant*] and of the "come back" [*reviens*] at the origin or end of every "come.")[12] The one, he or she, *who*ever it may be, to whom it is said "come," should not be determined in advance. For this absolute hospitality, it is the stranger, the *arrivant*. I shouldn't ask the absolute *arrivant* to start by stating his identity, by telling me who he is, under what circumstances I am going to offer him hospitality, whether he is going to be integrated or not, whether I am going to be able to "assimilate" him or not in my family, nation, or state. If he is an absolute *arrivant*, I shouldn't offer him any contract or impose any conditions upon him. I shouldn't, and moreover, by definition, I can't. This is why what looks like a morality of hospitality goes far beyond morality and above all beyond a right and a politics. Birth, which is similar to the thing I am trying to describe, may in fact not even be adequate to this absolute arrival [*arrivance*]. In families, it is prepared, conditioned, named in advance, drawn into a symbolic space which amortizes the arrival [*arrivance*]. And yet, despite these anticipations and pre-nominations, the element of chance [*l'aléa*] remains irreducible, the child who comes remains unforeseeable, it speaks, all by itself, as at the *origin* of another world, or at an *other* origin of this one.[13]

12

I have been struggling with this impossible concept, the messianic arrival [*arrivance*], for a long time. I have tried to elaborate its protocol at least, in *Aporias*[14] and *Specters of Marx*. The most difficult thing is to justify, at least provisionally, pedagogically, this predicate "messianic": it is a matter of an experience that is a priori messianic, but a priori exposed, in its very expectation, to what will be determined only a posteriori by the event. Desert in the desert (the one signaling toward the other), desert of a messianicity without messianism and therefore without doctrine and religious dogma, this arid and horizon-deprived expectation retains nothing of the great messianisms of the Book except the relation to an *arrivant* who may come – or never come – but of whom, by definition, I must know nothing in advance. Nothing, except that justice, in the most enigmatic sense of the word, is at stake. And, for the same reason, revolution, in that the event and justice are tied to this absolute rip in the foreseeable concatenation of historical time. The rip of eschatology in teleology, from which it must be dissociated here, which is always difficult. It is possible to renounce a certain revolutionary imagery or all revolutionary rhetoric, even to renounce a *certain* politics of revolution, so to speak, perhaps even to renounce every *politics* of revolution, but it is not possible to renounce revolution without also renouncing the event and justice.

The event cannot be reduced to the fact that something happens. It may rain tonight, it may not rain. This will not be an absolute event because I know what rain is, if in any case and insofar as I know what it is, and, moreover, this is not an absolutely other singularity. What happens or comes to pass in this case [*Ce qui arrive là*] is not an *arrivant*.

The *arrivant* must be absolutely other, an other that I expect not to be expecting, that I'm not waiting for, whose expectation is made of a nonexpectation, an expectation without what in philosophy is called a horizon of expectation, when a certain knowledge still anticipates and amortizes in advance. If I am sure that there is going to be an event, this will not be an event. It will be someone with whom I have an appointment, maybe the Messiah, maybe a friend, but if I know that he is coming, and if I am sure that he will come, then to this extent at least, this will not be an *arrivant*. But of course the arrival of someone I'm waiting for may also, in

13

another respect, surprise me every time like an unexpected bit of luck, something always new, and in this way happen to me again and again. Discreetly, in secret. And the *arrivant* may always not come, like Elijah. It is in the always-open hollow of this possibility, that is, in non-coming [*non-venue*], absolute disappointment [*déconvenue*], that I have a relation to the event: it is what may always not take place, too.

[. . .] On the basis of concerns that might well be deemed legitimate about economism or simply about the economic or even the monetary politics – even about the politics, period, in which the dominant European states are engaged – a certain left may suddenly find itself in positions of objective alliance with a nationalism or with an anti-Europeanism of the extreme right. At the moment, Le Pen[15] is placing great emphasis on his opposition to "free-trade-ism" or "economic libertarianism." This opportunistic rhetoric may make him the "objective ally," as we used to say, of those on the left who, for different reasons, are critical of the capitalist and monetaristic orthodoxy into which Europe is sinking. Only vigilance and clarity of acts, like vigilance and clarity of discourse, can dissolve these kinds of confusions, resolve them in analysis. The risk is constant, more serious than ever and, at times, "objectively" irreducible: for example, at election time. Even if one sharpens, as one should always try to, all the distinctions and dividing lines, in the reasons given for decisions and votes, in all the places of publication, demonstration, and action, in the end, on the occasion of a given electoral conjuncture (and given by whom, and how exactly?), the anti-European votes on the left and on the right get added together. The pro-European votes on the right and on the left too, for that matter. Similarly, there have been, as you know, revisionisms on the left – more specifically, and one should always be more specific, negationist revisionisms on the subject of the Holocaust – which have slipped insensibly into anti-Semitism (if, that is, they weren't inspired by it in the first place). Some of these revisionisms are fueled, more or less confusedly, by an a priori opposition to Israel or, even more precisely, by a rejection of the de facto politics of the state of Israel over the course of a very long period, and even over the course of Israel's entire history. Would these confusions stand up to honest and courageous analysis? One ought to be able to oppose *this* politics of *this* government of the state of Israel without a priori hostility to the existence of a state of Israel (and I would even say, on the contrary!), and without anti-Semitism and without anti-Zionism. I'll take this even further with another hypothesis: to go so far as to consider the historical foundation of this state itself, its conditions and its consequences, as cause for concern need not imply, not even on the part of certain Jews committed to the Zionist cause, a betrayal of Judaism. The logic of opposition to the state of Israel or to its de facto politics does not necessarily imply any anti-Semitism, or even any anti-Zionism, or above all any revisionism, in the sense I just specified. We could cite some very great examples here (such as Buber, in the past tense). Confining ourselves to principles and generalities, don't you think that, today, we have an obligation to denounce confusion, and to guard against it on *two sides*? There is, *on the one hand*, the nationalist confusion of those who slip from left to right by confusing every European project with the *fact* of the *current* [actuelle] politics of the European Community today, or the anti-Jewish confusion of those who fail to recognize the line dividing criticism of the state of Israel from opposition to a state of Israel as such, or from anti-Zionism, or from anti-Semitism, or from revisionism, etc. Here are at least five possibilities which ought to remain absolutely distinct. These metonymic slippings are all the more worrisome, politically, intellectually, and philosophically speaking, in that they threaten in this way, as it were from *both sides*, both those who succumb to them in practice and those who, *on the other hand*, denounce them while *symmetrically* espousing their logic. As if one could not do the one without doing the other, as if one could not oppose, for example, the current [*actuelle*] politics of Europe without being a priori anti-European, or as if one could not wonder about the state of Israel, about its past or present politics, even about the conditions of its foundation and a half-century of their consequences, without for all that being anti-Semitic, or even anti-Zionist, or again negationist-revisionist, etc. This *symmetry* of the adversaries allies obscurantist confusion with terrorism. It takes great determination and courage to resist these occult (occulting, occultist) strategies of amalgamation. If we want to stand up to this double maneuver of intimidation, the only responsible response is never to give up on distinctions and analyses. I would even say, never to give up on their Enlightenment, which is also to say, on the *public* demonstration of these distinctions (and this is not as easy as one might think). This resistance is all the more urgent now that we are in a phase where the critical reworking of this century's history is destined for troubled waters. We'll have to reread, reinterpret, dig up the archives, displace certain perspectives, etc. Where are we headed if all political critique and all historical reinterpretation ends up automatically associated with negationist-revisionism? If every question about the past or more generally about the constitution of the truth in history ends up accused of paving the way for revisionism? (I quote, in *Specters of Marx*, a particularly shocking example of this repressive idiocy that was printed in a major American newspaper.) What a victory for dogmatisms everywhere if anyone who tries to ask new questions, to upset good consciences or stereotypes, to complicate or reelaborate, in a new situation, the discourse of the left or the analysis of racism and of anti-Semitism, stands immediately accused of complicity with the adversary! Of course, in order to grant this trial as little purchase as possible, one must be twice as careful in public discourse, analyses, and interventions. And it is true that no absolute guarantee can ever be promised, and, still less, given. Recent examples could be used to illustrate the point still further, if further illustration were needed.

[. . .] Between the most general logics (the greatest predictability) and the most unpredictable singularities comes the intermediate schema of *rhythm*. For example, we had known since the 1950s what discredited and doomed the totalitarianisms of Europe and the East to failure. This was the daily bread of my generation (along with the old discourse, of the "Fukuyama" variety, on the supposed "end of history," on the "end of man," etc., which has been trotted out again today). What remained unpredictable was the rhythm, the speed, the date: for example, the date of the fall of the Berlin wall. In 1986–7, no one *in the world* could have had even an approximate idea of this date. Not that this rhythm is unintelligible. It can be analyzed after the fact when we take new causalities, which escaped experts at the time, into account (in the first place, the geopolitical effect of telecommunication in general: the entire sequence in which a signal such as, for example, the fall of the Berlin wall is inscribed would be impossible and unintelligible without a certain density of the tele-communications network, etc.).

[. . .] What I was just saying about the *arrivant* is politically unacceptable – if, at any rate, politics is based, which it always is, as such, on the idea of the identity of an inviolate body called the nation-state. There is not a single nation-state in the world today that is, as such, willing to say: "We open our doors to any and everyone. We place no limits on immigration." As far as I know [. . .] every nation-state is constituted through border control, through the refusal of illegal immigration, and through a strict limitation of the rights to immigration and asylum. The concept of the nation-state is constituted as much by the concept of the border as by the border itself.

From here, this concept can be treated in different ways, but these political differences, important as they may be, remain secondary with respect to the general political principle, namely, that the political is national. It authorizes the monitoring of border-crossings and the suppression of illegal immigration, even if it is acknowledged that this is in fact impossible and even, in certain economic conditions (an added hypocrisy), undesirable.

It would not be possible to derive a politics from what I was just saying about the absolute *arrivant*. Not in the traditional sense of the word "politics," not a politics that could be imple-mented by a nation-state. But without denying that what I was just saying about the event and the *arrivant* was, from the point of view of this concept of politics, an apolitical and inadmissible proposition, I would nonetheless argue that a politics that does not retain a reference to this principle of unconditional hospitality is a politics that loses its reference to justice. It may retain its right (which, here again, I distinguish from justice), the right to its right, but it loses justice. And the right to speak of it with any credibility. It would furthermore be necessary, although we can't get into it here, to try to distinguish between a politics of immigration and respect for the right of asylum. In principle, the right of asylum (such as it is recognized in France, for the time being, for political reasons) is paradoxically less political, since it need not be based [. . .] on the interests of the inviolate body of the nation-state that guarantees it. But beyond the fact that it is difficult to distinguish between the concepts of immigration and asylum, it is practically impossible to delimit the properly political nature of motives for exile, those which, in principle, in our Constitution, justify a request for asylum. After all, unemployment in a foreign country is a dysfunction of democracy and a kind of political persecution. What is more, and this, too, is the work of the market, rich countries are always partly responsible (even if only through interest on foreign debt and all that it symbolizes) for the politico-economic situations that force people into exile or emigration. Here, we come up against the limits of the political and the juridical: it will always be possible to show that, as such, a right of asylum may be null or infinite. This concept is therefore never rigorous, even if we wait for moments of global turmoil to worry about it. It would have to be thoroughly reelaborated if one wanted to understand or in some way change the current debate. (For example, between constitutionalism on the one hand and, on the other, the neopopulism of those who, like Mr Pasqua,[16] suddenly want to change the Constitution to adapt the article on the right of asylum to the alleged wishes of a new or very old "French people," which would all of a sudden no longer be the same "French people" that voted for its own Constitution.)

[. . .] The political class, the one in power after 1981 and the one that succeeds it today, is adapting less to xenophobia as such than to new possibilities for exploiting or abusing it by abusing the citizen. They are fighting over an electorate, grosso modo, that of the *"sécuritaires"*[17] (just as one says *"sanitaires"* – for it is indeed a question, they tell us, of the health and welfare of a social body around which is to be installed what they also call a "cordon sanitaire"), the electorate of the National Front, for whom a certain image of the quasi-biological hygiene of the inviolate national body is dominant. (Quasi-biological because the nationalist phantasm, like political rhetoric, often makes use of organicist analogies. I shall cite, by way of parenthetical example, the rhetoric of one of Le Pen's recent interventions, in *Le Monde*, August 24, 1993 – remarkable, as always, for its somnambulistic lucidity. To the classical idea of the territorial border as line of defense, Le Pen henceforth prefers the figure, at once apt and old-fashioned, of a "living membrane that admits only what is beneficial." If it were capable of calculating this filtration in advance, a living organism might achieve immortality, but in order to do so, it would have to die in advance, to let itself die or kill itself in advance, for fear of being *altered* by what comes from outside, by the other, period. Hence the theater of death to which racisms, biologisms, organicisms, eugenics are so often given, and sometimes philosophies of life. Before closing this parenthesis, let us underscore again what can't possibly make anyone happy: anyone, whether he is on the left or on the right, who, "like everybody," advocates immigration controls, bans illegal immigration, and would regulate the other, subscribes de facto and de jure, whether he likes it or not, with varying degrees of elegance or distinction, to Le Pen's organicist axiom, an axiom which is none other than that of a national front. (The front is a skin, a selective "membrane" admitting only the homogeneous or the homogenizable, the assimilable, or rather, that which is heterogeneous but considered to be "beneficial": the appropriable immigrant, the immigrant who is clean or proper.) We should not hide our eyes before this undeniable complicity. It is firmly rooted in the political insofar as it is bound up with and as long as it remains bound up with the nation-state. And when, like everybody, we have to acknowledge that we have no choice but to try to protect what we think is our inviolate body, when we want to regulate immigration and asylum (as they say they do, unanimously, on the left and on the right), we should at least not put on airs and give lessons in politics, in perfectly good conscience, by invoking grand principles. Just as Le Pen will always have the most extraordinary difficulty in justifying or adjusting the filtration of his "membrane," so there is, between all these allegedly opposed concepts and logics, a permeability that is more difficult to control than one often thinks or says: today, there is a neoprotectionism on the left and a neoprotectionism on the right, in economics as in matters of demographic flux, a free-trade-ism on the right and a free-trade-ism on the left, a neonationalism on the right and a neonationalism on the left. All these "neo" logics, too, cross, without any possible control, the protective membrane of their concepts to form shady alliances in discourse or in political and electoral acts. To acknowledge this permeability, this combinatory and its complicities, is not to take an apolitical position, nor is it to pronounce the end of the distinction between left and right or the "end of ideologies." On the contrary, it is to appeal to our

19

duty to courageously formulate and thematize this terrible combinatory, what is an indispensable preliminary not just to another
politics, to another discourse on the political, but to another
delimitation of the *socius* – specifically in relation to citizenship
and to nation-statehood in general, and more broadly, to identity
or subjectivity. It is hardly possible to talk about all this in an
interview and in parentheses. And yet [. . .] these problems are
anything but abstract or speculative today.)

[. . .] Why is the National Front able to exploit this fear or
exacerbate this impatience? Why, instead of taking the steps necessary to defuse this sentiment (pedagogy and socioeconomic
policy, etc.), are people trying either to appropriate the National
Front's theses or to exploit the division it is introducing in the so-
called republican right? All of this while the tide of immigration
has remained remarkably constant: it appears not to have changed
in decades and may even be decreasing. Do we find this surprising
or not? Analysis always tends to diminish surprise. We might
have expected as much, we say, after the fact, when we find the
element that escaped analysis, when we analyze otherwise (for
example, rising unemployment, the increasing permeability of
Europe's borders, the return, everywhere, of religions and of
identity-based religious, linguistic, and cultural claims within the
immigrant groups themselves; all this makes the same rate of
immigration seem more threatening to the self-identity of the host
social body). But an event that remains an event is an arrival, an
absolute arrival [*arrivance*]: it surprises and resists analysis after
the fact. At the birth of a child, the primal figure of the absolute
*arrivant*, you can analyze the causalities, the genealogical, genetic,
or symbolic premises, and all the wedding preparations you like.
Supposing this analysis could ever be exhausted, you will never
get rid of the element of chance [*l'aléa*], this place of the taking-
place, there will still be someone who speaks, someone irreplaceable, an absolute initiative, another origin of the world. Even if it
must dissolve in analysis or return to ash, it is an absolute spark.
The immigration of which France's history is made, the history of
its culture, religions, and languages, was first a history of these
children, children of immigrants or not, who were so many absolute
*arrivants*. The task of the philosopher, and thus of anyone – of the
citizen, for example – is to try, by taking the analysis as far as

possible, to make the event intelligible up until the moment we touch the *arrivant*. What is absolutely new is not one thing rather than another. It's the fact that something happens only once. It's what a date marks (a unique moment and a unique place), and it's always a birth or a death that a date dates. Even if the fall of the Berlin wall could have been foreseen, one day it happened, there were still deaths (before and during the collapse), and this is what makes it an ineffaceable event. It's birth and death that resist analysis: always the origin and end of the world. [. . .]

[. . .] It's better to let the future open – this is the axiom of deconstruction, the thing from which it always starts out and which binds it, like the future itself, to alterity, to the priceless *dignity* of alterity, that is to say, to justice. It is also democracy as democracy to come. You can imagine the objection. For example, someone will say: "Sometimes it's better that this or that thing not happen. Justice demands that certain events be prevented from happening (that certain '*arrivants*' be prevented from arriving or coming to pass). The event is not good in and of itself, the future is not unconditionally preferable." Granted, but it will always be possible to show that what we oppose, when we prefer, con-ditionally, that this or that thing not happen, is something that we think, rightly or wrongly, is going to obstruct the horizon – or even constitute the *horizon* (the word means *limit*) – for the absolute coming of the wholly other, for the future itself. There is, here, a messianic structure (if not a messianism – in my book on Marx, I also distinguish messianicity, as a universal dimension of experience, from all determinate messianisms) which knits the promise of the *arrivant*, the unanticipatability of the future, and justice inextricably together. I'm not able to reconstitute this demonstration here, and I realize that the word justice may seem a bit vague. It is not law or right – it both exceeds and founds human rights – nor is it distributive justice. It is not even respect, in the traditional sense of the word, for the other as *human subject*. It is the experience of the other as other, the fact that I let the other be other, which presupposes a gift without restitution, without reappropriation, and without jurisdiction. Here I cross, at the same time that I displace them slightly, as I've attempted to do else-where,[18] the heritages of several traditions: that of Levinas, when he simply defines the relation to the other as justice ("the relation

21

to the other – that is to say, justice"[19]); and that which insists through a paradoxical thought whose initially Plotinian formulation is found in Heidegger, then in Lacan: give not only what you have, but what you don't. This excess overflows the limits of the present, property, restitution, and no doubt law, morality, and politics, too, at the same time that it breathes life into or inspires them.

[. . .] Everything that heralded an Enlightenment philosophy, or inherited from it (not just rationalism, which does not necessarily come into it, but a progressivist, teleological, humanist, critical rationalism) fights [. . .] a "return of the worst," which teaching and awareness of the past are supposed to be able to prevent. Although this Enlightenment battle often takes the form of a conjuration or denial, we have no choice but to join in the struggle and reaffirm this philosophy of emancipation. Personally, I believe in its future, and I have never felt that all those declarations about the end of the great emancipatory or revolutionary discourses were true. Still, their very affirmation testifies to the *possibility* of what they oppose: the return of the worst, an ineducable repetition compulsion in the death drive and radical evil, a history without progress, a history without history, etc. And the Enlightenment of our time cannot be reduced to that of the eighteenth century. Another, still more radical way for philosophy to "struggle" with the return of the worst consists in disavowing (denying, exorcising, conjuring or warding off, each mode would have to be analyzed) what this recurrence of evil may well be made of: a law of the spectral, which resists an ontology (the phantom or ghost [*le revenant*] is neither present nor absent, it neither is nor is not, nor can it be dialecticized) as well as a philosophy of the subject, of the object, or of consciousness (of being-present) – consciousness, which is also destined, like ontology or like philosophy itself, to "chase after" specters, to chase them out or hunt them down. Thus it also consists in failing to understand certain psychoanalytic lessons about the phantom, but also about the repetition of the worst, which threatens all historical progress. To which I will add, too quickly, on the one hand, that it only threatens a certain concept of progress, and that there would be no progress, in general, without this threat; and, on the other hand, that there is, in what has dominated psychoanalytic discourse up to now, starting with Freud, a certain disavowal of the spectral structure and logic – a powerful, subtle, unstable disavowal which it nonetheless shares with science and with philosophy. Yes, a ghost can come back, like the worst, but without this possible coming-back, and if we refuse to acknowledge its irreducible originality, we are deprived of memory, heritage, justice, of everything that has value beyond life and by which the dignity of life is measured. I have tried to suggest this elsewhere and am having trouble schematizing it here.

[...] What happened in France well before, and during, the Second World War and even more so, I would say, during the war in Algeria, superimposed, and therefore overdetermined, strata of forgetting. This accumulation of silence is particularly opaque, resistant, and dangerous. Slowly, discontinuously, in a contradictory way, this pact of secrecy is giving way to a movement of the liberation of memory (especially of public memory, so to speak, of its official legitimation, which never advances at the rhythm of historical knowledge, nor at that of private memory, if there is such a thing and if it is purely private). But if this breaking of the seal is contradictory, both in its effects and in its motivation, this is precisely because of the phantom. Even as we remember the worst (out of respect for memory, the truth, the victims, etc.), the worst threatens to return. One phantom recalls another. And it is often because we see signs announcing the resurgence or the quasi-resurrection of the one that we appeal to the other. We remember how urgent it is to commemorate, officially, the roundup of the Jews in the Vel d'Hiv,[20] or to declare a certain responsibility on the part of the French state for what happened of "the worst" under the Occupation, at the moment when (and because) signs are announcing this return – in a totally different context, sometimes with the same face, sometimes a different one – of nationalism, of racism, of xenophobia, of anti-Semitism. The two memories bolster, aggravate, and conjure one another; they are, necessarily, again and again, at war. Always on the brink of every possible kind of contamination. When abhorred ghosts, so to speak, are back, we recall the ghosts of their victims. We remember them in order to preserve their memory, but also, indissociably, we call them back for our struggle today and, above all, for the promise that binds it, for the future, without which it would make no sense: for the future, that is to say, beyond all present life, beyond any living being capable of saying "now, me." The question – or the demand – of the phantom is the question and the demand of the future and of justice as well. This double return encourages an irrepressible tendency toward confusion. We confuse the analogous with the identical: "Exactly the same thing is repeating itself, exactly the same thing." No, a certain iterability (difference in repetition) ensures that what comes back nevertheless remains a wholly other event. A phantom's return is, each time, another, different return, on a different stage, in new conditions to which we must always pay the closest attention if we don't want to say or do just anything.

Yesterday, a German journalist calls me on the telephone (to talk about this "call" of European intellectuals "to vigilance," which I, like others, felt it was my duty to sign, about which and around which there would be so much to say – but we don't have enough time to do it seriously). Observing that, for obvious reasons, many German intellectuals had applauded this gesture and judged it opportune, particularly in Germany's current [*actuelle*] situation, she wondered if there wasn't, in all of this, a return to the tradition of a "J'accuse." Where is Zola today? she asked. I tried to explain why, despite my immense respect for Zola, I am not sure that his is the only or the best model for a "J'accuse" that might take place today. Everything has changed – public space, the paths traced by information and decision, the relationship between power and secrecy, the figures of the intellectual, the writer, the journalist, etc. It's not the "J'accuse" that is outdated, but the form and space of its inscription. Of course we should remember the Dreyfus affair, but we should also know that it can't be repeated as such. Something worse may happen, we can never rule this out, but not the Dreyfus affair as such.

In short, in order to think (but what, then, does "thinking" mean?) [...] the "return of the worst," it would therefore be necessary to take up, beyond ontology, beyond a philosophy of life or of death, beyond a logic of the conscious subject, the relations between politics, history, and the ghost [*le revenant*] ...

In *Specters of Marx*, I open [...] a critical dialogue with Marx's text, guided by the question of the specter (as it crosses those of repetition, of mourning, of inheritance, of the event, and of messianicity, of everything that exceeds the ontological oppositions between absence and presence, the visible and the invisible, the living and the dead, and, thus, above all, the question of the prosthesis as "phantom member," the question of technics [*la technique*], of the teletechnological simulacrum, of the computer-generated image, of virtual space, etc. – again we encounter the themes we talked about earlier, of *artifactuality* and of *virtuactuality*). You will recall the first sentence of the *Communist Manifesto*: "A specter is haunting Europe today, the specter of communism." I investigate, I prowl around a bit with all the specters who, literally, obsess Marx. There is, here, a persecution *of* Marx. He pursues them everywhere, hunts them, but they, too, are on his tracks: in the *Eighteenth Brumaire*, in *Capital*, but above all in the *German Ideology*, which mounts [. . .] an interminable critique – interminable because fascinated, captivated, spellbound – of the Stirnerian obsession [*hantise*], a hallucination which is itself already critical, and which Marx has a good deal of trouble shaking off.

I try to decipher this logic of the spectral in Marx's work. I propose to do it with respect, so to speak, to what is going on in the world today, in a new public space transformed as much by what is quickly called the "return of the religious" as by teletechnologies. What is the work of mourning concerning Marxism? What does it seek to *conjure*? The very ambiguous word and concept of *conjuration* (in at least three languages: French, English, and German) play a role as important as those of inheritance in this essay. To inherit is not essentially to *receive* something, a *given* that one may then *have*. It is an active affirmation, it answers an injunction, but it also presupposes initiative, it presupposes the signature or countersignature of a critical selection. When one inherits, one sorts, one sifts, one reclaims, one reactivates. I also believe, although I'm not able to demonstrate it here, that every assignation of an inheritance harbors a contradiction and a secret. (This is something like the organizing idea of this book, which links Marx's genius to that of Shakespeare – whom Marx loved so much and cites so often, especially *Timon of Athens* and *Much Ado about Nothing* – as well as to Hamlet's father, who could be the essay's capital character.)

Hypothesis: there is always more than one spirit. Whenever one speaks of spirit one immediately evokes spirits, specters, and whoever inherits chooses one spirit over another. One selects, one filters, one sifts through ghosts or through the injunctions of each spirit. Only when the assignations are multiple and contradictory is there inheritance, only when they are secret enough to challenge interpretation, to call for the limitless risk of active interpretation. Only then is there a decision and a responsibility to be taken or made. When there is no *double-bind* [in English in the original], there is no responsibility. Inheritance must retain an undecidable reserve . . .

If to inherit is to reaffirm an injunction, not simply a possession, but an assignation to be deciphered, then we are only what we inherit. Our being is inheritance, the language we speak is inheritance. Hölderlin basically says that we were given language so that we might bear witness to that whose heritage we are. Not the heritage we have or receive, but the heritage we are, through and through. What we are, we inherit. And we inherit language, which we use to bear witness to the fact that we are what we inherit. It is a paradoxical circle within which we must struggle and settle things by decisions which at one and the same time inherit and invent – necessarily in the absence of stable norms, of programs – their own norms. To say that inheritance is not a good that we receive, to remember that we are inheritors through and through is, therefore, in no way traditionalist or backward-looking. We are, among other things, inheritors of Marx and of Marxism. I try to explain why this is an event that no one and nothing can efface, not even – especially not – the totalitarian monstrosity. (Of totalitarianisms, there were more than one, all of which were in some way linked to Marxism, none of which can be interpreted simply as perversions or distortions of its heritage.) And even people who haven't read Marx, or who have never so much as heard his name, even anticommunists or anti-Marxists are inheritors of Marx. And then, it is not possible to inherit from Marx without also inheriting from Shakespeare, without inheriting from the Bible and from quite a few other things, too.

[. . .] I don't believe in the return of communism in the dominant form of the party (the party form is doubtless on its way to extinction, more generally, in political life, it is an afterlife that may last a long time, of course), nor in the return of everything that discouraged us from a certain Marxism and from a certain communism. I hope this doesn't come back, it's almost certain that it won't, and we should in any case make sure that it doesn't. But for this same insurrection in the name of justice to give rise to critiques that are Marxist in *inspiration*, Marxist in *spirit* – this cannot fail to happen again. There are signs of it. It is like a new International without party, without organization, without association. It is searching, it is hurting, it thinks that things are not OK, it does not accept the new "world order" that some are in the process of trying to impose, it finds the discourse inspired by this new order sinister. This insurrectional restlessness will recover from Marxist inspiration forces for which we have no names. Although it sometimes seems to have elements of a *critique*, I try to explain why it's not, why it shouldn't be merely a critique, a method, a theory, a philosophy, or an ontology. It would take a completely different form and would perhaps call for reading Marx in a completely different way. But it's not a matter of reading in the philological or academic sense. It's not a matter of rehabilitating a Marxist canon. A certain vogue, with which I take issue in this essay, might well be in the process of slowly neutralizing Marx in yet another way. Now that Marxism is dead and the Marxist apparatus has been dismantled, they would say, we will be able to read *Capital* and to read Marx quietly, theoretically, we will be able to grant him the legitimacy he deserves as a great philosopher whose writings belong (in their "internal intelligibility," as Michel Henry puts it) to the great ontological tradition. No, I try to explain why we ought not to be content with this pacifying rereading. [. . .]

# ECHOGRAPHIES OF
# TELEVISION

*JACQUES DERRIDA AND
BERNARD STIEGLER*

With the exception of a few very slight modifications (changes in the length or punctuation of a sentence, the addition of a brief note clarifying a context, the division into chapters, each bearing a title), this text corresponds to the full and literal transcription of an improvised interview shot by Jean-Christophe Rosé under the auspices of the INA (Institut National de l'Audiovisuel), on Wednesday, December 22, 1993.

# 1

# RIGHT OF INSPECTION

BERNARD STIEGLER   *When I first came to you with the idea for this recording, you asked that the conditions of its use be clearly defined. You wished, in particular, to exercise your right of inspection [droit de regard] over the use that might be made of the images we are recording at this very moment. Could you explain your reasons for making this request? Much more generally, what would a "right of inspection" be in the era of television and of what you recently dubbed "teletechnologies"?*

JACQUES DERRIDA   If I made such a request, if I voiced it *in principle and in general*, it was, first of all, without any great illusion. Without any illusion as to the effectiveness of such a "right of inspection." But in order to recall, precisely, its principle. We know it is impossible to control these things. It is already impossible in the domain of publication, where "intellectuals" and writers would be "more at home," as it were, under cover of the written. Control of written publication is already difficult; it is a fortiori when we are talking about cameras, film, and television. And so, if I wished to have this right of inspection, it was without any illusion, but also without any protectionist or inquisitorial anxiety. It was simply to reaffirm a principle, that is to say, to have the opportunity to *state* this *principle*, to *propose* it. Like many others, I think that one of the problems experienced, really by anyone who expresses himself in front of a camera, but particularly by intellectuals, teachers or writers, who are concerned to prepare or watch what they say or to proceed with caution, one of these problems which can turn into a political drama, is that

31

they feel enjoined by a contradictory injunction: they must not refuse to bear witness or cut themselves off from the public sphere, which is dominated, today, by television in general, but at the same time, they are less than they are elsewhere in a position – I won't say to appropriate – but in any case to adapt the conditions of production, of recording, of what we're in the process of doing here and now, in such artificial conditions, to their own requirements. And I'm not even talking about broadcast or distribution yet.

Already, I have the impression that our control is very limited. I am *at home* [chez moi],[1] but with all these machines and all these prostheses watching, surrounding, seducing us, the quote "natural" conditions of expression, discussion, reflection, deliberation are to a large extent breached, falsified, warped. One's first impulse would therefore be to at least try to reconstitute the conditions in which one would be able to say what one wants to say at the rhythm at which and in the conditions in which one wants to say it. And has the right to say it. And in the ways that would be least inappropriate. This is always difficult. It is *never* purely and simply possible, but it is *particularly* difficult in front of the camera. What is more, the "home" [*le "chez-soi"*] to which I just alluded in passing (the *casa* hidden in the *etymon* of this little word "*chez*") is no doubt what is most violently affected by the intrusion, in truth by the breaking and entering [*l'effraction*] of the telepowers we're getting ready to talk about here – as violently injured, moreover, as the historical distinction (it is old, but not natural and not timeless) between public and private space.

What I would have liked to convey by this illusionless request is the paradox of a task or a watchword: perhaps it is necessary to fight, today, *not against* teletechnologies, television, radio, e-mail or the Internet but, on the contrary, so that the development of these media will make more room for the norms that a number of citizens would be well within their rights to propose, affirm, and lay claim to – particularly those "intellectuals," artists, writers, philosophers, analysts, scientists, certain journalists and media professionals, too, who would like to say something about the media or analyze them at the same rhythm at which we are trying to do this together, here and now. That's all I wanted to suggest.

The expression you used at the end of your question, "right of inspection," is obviously a very ambiguous one. It may refer to abusive authority, authority which has been usurped, violently appropriated or imposed in a situation where we don't "naturally" have any rights. The law of inspection is furthermore in itself an authority against which one might revolt. Who has right of inspection over whom? Right, every right, in a certain sense, is right of inspection, every right gives the right of inspection. Right equals "right of inspection." Kant reminded us of this, that there is no right without the ability to exercise the force that will ensure it is respected. Thus there is no right that does not consist in conferring upon a power a right to control and surveillance and, therefore, a right of inspection, in a situation where nothing guarantees it "naturally."

But in the context in which you raised it, you wanted to know, in a general way, what links the juridical, or the juridico-political, to seeing, to vision, but also to the capture of images, to their use. It remains a question as to who, in the end, is authorized to appear

33

[*se montrer*] but above all authorized to show [*montrer*], edit, store, interpret, and exploit images. It is a timeless question, but it is taking on original dimensions today. One would have to approach this specificity via the very general question of the right of inspection, which exceeds both our time and our culture. We are not going to go into this vast question, which would take us back to the Bible, to Plato or even to the question of the gaze [*le regard*] in other cultures. But even if we confine ourselves to framing this question exclusively in terms of our time and in terms of the technology of images, there is much to do. There is much to say, whether about the right to *penetrate* a "public" or "private" space, the right to "introduce" the eye and all these optical prostheses (movie cameras, still cameras, etc.) into the "home" of the other, or whether about the right to know who owns, who is able to appropriate, who is able to select, who is able to show images, directly political or not. I had used this expression, "right of inspection," in reference to photography, to a mute photographic work,[2] the narrative matrices of which I had multiplied, but it goes far beyond the question of art – or of photography as art. It concerns everything that, in public space today, is regulated by the production and circulation of images, real or virtual, and thus of gazes, eyes, optical prostheses, etc.

*It is also an institutional question and a question of the right of access to archival images.*

Yes.

*I'm thinking, in this instance, of a text that was published in* Le Monde *last October, which you signed, concerning the enforcement of a law passed by Parliament in 1992, instituting the* "dépôt légal"[3] *of film and television programming, that is to say, film and television archives, and opening these archives to researchers. This access had previously been barred by economic as well as by juridical law: there was no obligation to make these image and sound recordings available to researchers. Now there is a law, which ought to be in force but isn't yet.*[4]

As soon as this law exists (the question of its enforcement, serious as it may be, being for the moment secondary), it acknowledges that society, a state or a nation, has the right or duty to "store" ["*stocker*"], to preserve [*mettre en réserve*] the quasi-totality of what is produced and broadcast on national stations. Once this has been preserved, accumulated, ordered, classed, the law should grant access to it, as to all patrimony, as to all national property. And it should extend this access to *every* citizen who wants to consult this archive. (*At least* to every citizen, for this enormous question of right cannot necessarily be limited to the citizen and to the right or law of a nation-state as such. Everything that is affecting, and this is not nothing, the juridical concept of the state's sovereignty today has a relation – an essential relation – *to* the media and is at times conditioned *by* the telepowers and teleknowledges we're talking about. What is more, all states do not have the same history and the same politics of the national archive. They all have a different concept of the access that should be extended to noncitizens.)

I imagine that if there was some hesitation or a period of latency before this law could even be produced and, after that, enforced, this is because, in the end, this new type of archive creates original problems. The norms that had already been adopted for other types of repositories [*mémoires*] or archives, for example, the written archive, the *dépôt légal* of books, wound up getting displaced by the enormous production of the radiophonic or televisual archive. It seems that no limit should be placed on the access of citizens to this archive – nor, for that matter, I just alluded to it, on that of foreigners. It's actually a matter of something that is already public, that has already been put out there, already been shown. There is no secret here, no reason of state can be invoked. Consequently, it is completely normal for the state to guarantee, without delay, to anyone who wants to study these public documents – one thinks first of researchers and of research that ought to be developed in the audiovisual domain – not only the formal right, but the technical conditions of access to this archive. If the enforcement of this law has been delayed, this is unacceptable. That's why a certain number of us protested what was due, perhaps, as the government has claimed, to techno-empirical reasons, perhaps to less "neutral" reasons, let's leave this question aside for the moment. In any case, the delay in this domain is a violation of the right of anyone who wants to consult a public archive.

All the more so as this is becoming a particularly urgent area of research, obviously for theoretical, philosophical, scientific, and historical reasons – the task of the historian intersects, here, all the others – but for political reasons too. For we now know the effect that the production and, subsequently, the broadcast or distribution of discourse or of images can have on public space. It is all too clear today, the political arena is to a large extent marked and, often, determined, well beyond the usual places, well beyond the statutory organs of political debate and decision-making (Parliament, the government, etc.), by what is being aired on the radio or shown on television. The fact of having access to these archives, of being able to analyze their content and the modalities of selection, interpretation, manipulation that superintended their production and circulation, all these things are therefore a citizen's right. Again, I say "citizen" in a way that's a bit vague for the moment. No doubt we'll have a chance to come back to this. I think this right should be the right, not only of the citizen of a state, but also of "foreigners." A new ethics and a new law or right, in truth, a new concept of "hospitality" are at stake. What the accelerated development of teletechnologies, of cyberspace, of the new topology of "the virtual" is producing is a practical *deconstruction* of the traditional and dominant concepts of the state and citizen (and thus of "the political") as they are linked to the actuality of a territory. I say "deconstruction" because, ultimately, what I name and try to think under this word is, at bottom, nothing other than this very process, its "taking-place" in such a way that its happening affects the very experience of place, and the recording (symptomatic, scientific, or philosophical) of this "thing," the trace that traces (inscribes, preserves, carries, refers, or defers) the différance of this event which happens to place [*qui arrive au lieu*] – which happens to take place, and to taking-place [*qui arrive à (l')avoir-lieu*] . . .

*Television belongs to the contemporary apparatus of teletechnologies, which is obviously much more complex than television alone. It is possible to read you and to understand that writing – any form of writing – is already a kind of teletechnology. The power to address a letter is a sending away from oneself which already breaks the circle of any proximity, of any immediacy,*

36

*and you have indeed shown that there is in fact never any immedi-*
*ate proximity, that there is always already something like a writing*
*and therefore like a teletechnology. What, then, would be the speci-*
*ficity of what you have recently given this name"teletechnology"?*
*A moment ago, you said that you have no illusions as to the*
*control we might hope to have over the operation in which we*
*are now engaged, for example, or over its destination. And you*
*reminded us that you had already said, about writing, that there*
*is no possible mastery of its "meaning" ["vouloir-dire"]. How do*
*contemporary teletechnologies, and especially television, bring up*
*the problem of this nonmastery in a singular way?*

As always, the choice is not *between* mastery and nonmastery,
any more than it is *between* writing and nonwriting in the everyday sense. The way in which I had tried to define writing implied
that it was already, as you noted, a teletechnology, with all that
this entails of an original expropriation. The choice does not choose
between control and noncontrol, mastery and nonmastery, property or expropriation. What is at stake here, and it obeys another
"logic," is rather a "choice" between multiple configurations of
mastery without mastery (what I have proposed to call *"exappropriation"*). But it also takes the phenomenal form of a war, a
conflictual tension between multiple forces of appropriation,
between multiple strategies of control. Even if no one can ever
control everything, it is a question of knowing whom you want to
restrict, by what and by whom you don't want what you say or
what you do to be immediately and totally reappropriated. I'm
not under any illusion about the possibility of my controlling or
appropriating what I do, what I say or what I am, but I do want
– this is the point of every struggle, of every drive in this domain
– I would at least like the things I say and do not to be immediately and clearly used toward ends I feel I must oppose. I don't
want to reappropriate my product, but for the same reason,
I don't want others doing this toward ends I feel I must fight. It's
a struggle, really, between multiple movements of appropriation,
or of exappropriation, an illusionless struggle precisely because it
gets displaced between two equally inaccessible poles.

That said, what, in terms of the general history of teletechnology or of teletechnological writing, is the specificity of our

moment, with devices like those that surround us here? This is an enormous and difficult question. The specificity of this moment has forms and folds that we can't describe or analyze now in the way that would be required if we had the time: if we weren't in the present situation of televised recording. We must consequently try both to mark the fact that we aren't able to speak here in the way that we are used to speaking and writing about these subjects, we must try not to efface this constraint, and at the same time, to respect the specificity of this situation in order to address these questions, in the moment, with another rhythm and in another style.

So perhaps we should begin by saying the following, which is still very general: this specificity, whatever it may be, does not all of a sudden substitute the prosthesis, teletechnology, etc., for immediate or natural speech. These machines have always been there, they are always there, even when we wrote by hand, even during so-called live conversation. And yet, the greatest compatibility, the greatest coordination, the most vivid of possible affinities seems to be asserting itself, *today*, between what appears to be most alive, most *live* [in English in the original],[5] and the différance or delay, the time it takes to exploit, broadcast, or distribute it. When a scribe or an eighteenth- or nineteenth-century writer wrote, the moment of inscription was not kept alive. The material support, the forms of inscription were preserved, but no "living" or supposedly living trace of the writer, of his face, his voice, his hand, etc. At the opposite extreme, now, at this very instant, we are living a very singular, unrepeatable moment, which you and I will remember as a contingent moment, which took place only once, of something that was live, that is live, that we think is simply live, but that will be reproduced *as live*, with a reference to this present and this moment anywhere and anytime, weeks or years from now, reinscribed in other frames or "contexts." A maximum of "tele," that is to say, of distance, lag, or delay, will convey what will continue to stay alive, or rather, the immediate image, the living image of the living: the timbre of our voices, our appearance, our gaze, the movement of our hands. It is a simple and poignant thing that, until the end of the nineteenth century, not one singer's voice could be recorded. No one's voice could be recorded in its "own movement"! Not even the voices of people

38

whose archives we felt obliged to keep public (singers but also writers, storytellers, orators, politicians, etc.).

Well, precisely because we know now, under the lights, in front of the camera, listening to the echo of our own voices, that this *live* [in English] moment will be able to be – that it is already – captured by machines that will transport and perhaps show it God knows when and God knows where, we already know that death is here. The INA is a machine, and this machine works like a kind of undertaker, recording things and archiving moments about which we know a priori that, no matter how soon after their recording we die, and even if we were to die while recording, *voilà*, this will be and will remain "live," a simulacrum of life. A maximum of life (the most life [*le plus de vie*]), but of life that already yields to death ("no more life" [*"plus de vie"*]), this is what becomes exportable for the longest possible time and across the greatest possible distance – but in a finite way. It is not inscribed for eternity, for it is finite, and not just because the subjects are finite, but because the archive we're talking about, too, can be destroyed. The greatest intensity of "live" life is captured from as close as possible in order to be borne as far as possible away. If there is a specificity, it stems from the measure of this distance, it stems from this polarity which holds together the closest and the farthest away. This polarity already existed, with the quote most "archaic" or most "primitive" writing, but today it is taking on a dimension out of all proportion with what it was before. Of course, we should not define a specificity by a quantitative difference. And so we would have to find structural differences – and I think there are some, for example, this restitution as "living present" of what is dead – within this acceleration or amplification, which seem incommensurable, incomparable with all that preceded them for millions of years.

*Isn't the possibility of live transmission, for example – we might very well imagine that the image being captured by the camera at this very moment was being broadcast immediately – something which marks an absolute specificity as compared to writing?*

One might be tempted to think so. There is certainly what is called live transmission, the transport, by "reportage," of political events, for example, or of a war. There have been many recent examples of this. Although this supposed "live" does in fact introduce a considerable structural innovation into the space we're talking about, we should never forget that this "live" is not an absolute "live," but only a live effect [*un effet de direct*], an allegation of "live." Whatever the apparent immediacy of the transmission or broadcast, it negotiates with choices, with framing, with selectivity. In a fraction of a second, CNN, for example, intervenes to select, censor, frame, filter the so-called "live" [in English] or "direct" image. To say nothing of programming decisions, whether with regard to what is "shown" or who "shows" or manipulates it. What is "transmitted" "live" on a television channel is *produced before being transmitted*. The "image" is not a faithful and integral reproduction of what it is thought to reproduce. Still less of everything that remains "reproducible." This would hold equally for the modest experiment that we are conducting here. Suppose that what we are in the process of recording were to be viewed somewhere else, at this very moment, for example in another country, where all our allusions to the "French scene" today would most likely be unintelligible. Everything would be subject to a distortion, consequently introducing delays and supplementary interpretations. Nor is it even necessary to invoke a foreign country for this. When it is a question of more politically charged events – a battle, a parliamentary debate, a military or humanitarian intervention, the live retransmission, no matter how direct it "technically" appears, is immediately caught in a web of all kinds of interventions. It is framed, cut, it begins here, is interrupted there. We might describe ad infinitum all these modes of intervention which ensure that the "live," the "direct," is never intact. That this technical possibility exists, however limited, impure, "fictional" it may be, is enough, to be sure, to change our understanding of the entire field. As soon as we know, "believe we know," or quite simply *believe* that the alleged "live" or "direct" is possible, and that voices and images can be transmitted from one side of the globe to the other, the field of perception and of experience in general is profoundly transformed.

# 2

# ARTIFACTUALITY, HOMOHEGEMONY

BERNARD STIEGLER   *In an interview which you granted to the journal* Passages,[1] *you said that time, that is to say, in this case, the time of public speech, is an artifact. "Public space . . . [is] a political present. At every moment, this political present is transformed, in its structure and in its content, by the teletechnology of what is so confusedly called information or communication." Actuality, then, is made, and this is why you speak of "artifactuality." This means, first of all, as you just now described it, that it results from a process of selection, that it is "not given but actively produced, sifted, invested, performatively interpreted by numerous devices which are* factitious *or* artificial, *hierarchizing and selective." And you added: "Actuality comes to us by way of a fictional fashioning." This selective production is simultaneously a system of capture, of treatment, of distribution, and of conservation, at least. Consequently, it corresponds to a criteriology. You speak several times, in different works and especially in your recent book* Specters of Marx, *of the need for a politics of memory. In what would this politics consist, particularly with regard to this selectivity? This selection, which is in memory in general in all its forms, is irreducible. The problem is not that the artifactuality of what we might call the "memory industries" selects. The problem is that of the criteria for this selection. If it is true that this criteriology is overdetermined by the commercial character of industry, and so governed by the principle of a realization of surplus-values, are we talking, by a politics of memory, about regulating the effects that a hegemonic market pressure can have on the construction of actuality?*

41

JACQUES DERRIDA   This is a series of very difficult questions. This portmanteau word, "artifactuality," signifies first of all that there is *actuality* – in the sense of "what is timely" [*"ce qui est actuel"*] or rather, in the sense of "what is broadcast under the heading of *the news* [*sous le titre d'*actualités] on radio and television" – only insofar as a whole set of technical and political apparatuses come as it were to choose, from a nonfinite mass of events, the "facts" that are to constitute actuality: what are then called "the facts" on which the "news" or "information" feeds. This is all banal, too well known, even if it is easily forgotten, and this interpretive sifting is not confined to the news or the media. It is indispensable at the threshold of every perception or of every finite experience in general.

The choices, of course, are never neutral, whether they are made at the television and radio stations or whether they are already decided at the press agencies. All actuality negotiates with the artifice, in general dissimulated, of this filtration. But already it should be added – I note it so that I can move as quickly as possible to your last question – that these artifices are controlled, simultaneously or alternately, by private or by state agencies. This is in order to approach the question of the market, which you raised a moment ago. Currently, in order to palliate a state hegemony, whose effects on artifactuality have naturally been feared, radio and television institutions are being opened to the market. This does not mean that public channels are outside the market, however. They must yield to the market in their turn. More than ever.

What is the market, in this case? One might at first be tempted to oppose a market to a state practice, and to think that public channels are outside the market. We know this is in no way the case. The one thing we can't do today is delimit the market. We know that, once they are in competition with private channels or stations, public institutions must conquer the market, open themselves to advertising, and work with a view to the ratings [*l'Audimat*].[2] At that moment, nothing escapes the market or what you call surplus-value.

One must then re-pose the enormous problem of knowing what can be inscribed in the market or exceed the market in this respect. It is not enough to remember that, today, television journalists, like politicians, speak with a prompter in front of them. One must know that there are now machines that can, at any given moment, advise the journalist in charge of a program of fluctuations in the ratings from one sentence to the next. From one sentence to the next, he must in principle be ready to take the market into account, or to take into account what the ratings translate from the current state of the audience, which must be reckoned with if the advertising is going to be profitable, if the channel is going to be "competitive," etc. What are we to make of the interposition of this text that someone reads while pretending to look straight into the eye of a viewer whom he or she can't see and who, in turn, can't see that the person addressing him may at the same time be in the process of reading from a prompter and of following the evolution of the ratings? It's as if the newscaster were reading the artifact called "Audimat" on the face of an anonymous, artificial, unconscious, abstract, virtual, spectral interlocutor: "ourselves," "the others," we who order everything without knowing, like animals, machines, or gods.

This imperative of the market, which the state itself must reckon with, is therefore one of the determining elements – I won't say *the* determining element, "in the last instance" – of this artifactuality. In order to deal seriously with this question (but can we even do this in these conditions?), one would have to know what the market, free trade, the national market, and above all, the international market are, since these problems are at the very heart of an actuality that has been what is called "globalized" in terms of the circulation of televisual commodities from one country to another, from one nation-state to another, from one cultural or political zone (United States/European Union for example) or from one linguistic zone (Americano-Anglophone/Francophone for example) to another. All these questions are absolutely indissociable from one another, and they would have to be taken up. Is this possible in the time we have here, at this rhythm and in these conditions?

*Well, that's precisely it. Does it seem conceivable to you that the market could be regulated by something that would negotiate with the law of the market, but that would nevertheless not simply submit to it? You just raised the question of what has been called the "cultural exception,"[3] which refers to a question of territory, to its confrontation with the nonterritoriality of the image today. But I'm also thinking of a legal case that seems to me to be a very powerful index, what has been called the "Grégory affair."[4] Recently, the media have been indulging in a kind of self-affirmation of guilt about this. And one may indeed wonder with respect to this example whether, by playing with the sensational character of events, the market has not acquired a power so great that the very principles of law have been radically disrupted, to the point where the process of preliminary examination[5] has been compromised as a result. The market seems to have utterly exceeded its sphere by unsettling the very conditions of the exercise of law. What is more, a few years ago, Marguerite Duras intervened in this case, and now the Villemins are filing a suit against her. Here, we are no longer simply dealing with the question of the market, nor simply with the fiction that the media story in some sense always entails, but with a literary gesture getting inscribed or mixed up in the domain of the media and in one way or another playing with the "market." Does it seem possible to you, then, to regulate this market – which would not necessarily exempt us from having to negotiate with it – in order to prevent it from becoming an absolutely hegemonic law, which would constitute a danger to democracy and to the exercise of law or right?*

One of the many difficulties here stems from this concept of the market, from *this* market and from this kind of commodity. Sometimes it seems as if we're talking, under this word, about a field of economic interests, of productions of values or of surplus-values, etc., sometimes it seems as if we're simply talking about public space. One mustn't, under the pretext of regulating the market, place limits on the publicness of public space. These two things, which are not to be confused, are often inextricably intertwined. There is always a risk of limiting citizens' access to public speech under the pretext of limiting the market effect. What happens in the press, on radio and television, is *at one and the same time* the market and the condition of what is called democracy, the condition of the free expression of any and everyone about anything or anyone in the public space. It is therefore necessary to really determine what belongs to the market – if there is one in the strict sense – and, on the other hand, what belongs to the openness of public space (in which it would also be necessary to distinguish the limits of a "civic space"). One certainly gets the sense that "regulating the market," to use your expression, may in certain cases lead, perhaps the state, perhaps, even more worrisome, collections of private forces which the state sometimes represents, to limit the free circulation and free production of speech, works, etc., to the benefit, once again, of a place of private appropriation. In passing, you mentioned the "cultural exception." I don't feel capable of intervening in this debate on the terms in which it has been framed. I am able to see what, in the two logics that confront each other (that are, one might say, in competition!), may be legitimate, given the premises of this debate. One logic consists in saying, not in the name of the market, but in the name of the free development of inventive productions (in a public space which cannot be reduced to civic and national space), that we must not close borders and reserve priority or exclusivity for national production. This could actually promote a mediocre production, as long as it is national, to the detriment of a foreign production which would be more interesting, and to which citizens also have the right to have access. One can certainly understand the logic of this openness of borders, and the need for lifting every cultural exception. Conversely, if the openness of these borders means that powerful machines of industrial production are able to flood the market with homogenizing, mediocre products, isn't it better to resist this strictly commercial hegemony? But in this case, perhaps one would have to fight, not with the weapons of nationalist protection, but by supporting or appealing to the production of works capable of withstanding competition, and of surviving it not simply because the "works" assert themselves by virtue of their force, their necessity, their "genius" (an equally indispensable condition), but because the field of reception and the nature of demand has changed. This would have to happen through a general transformation of civil society, of the state, and for example, where the two cross, a corresponding transformation of the school or of education. This is very difficult, almost unimaginable. In each case, the strategy may be different, and I don't think that the decision of this matter, if there could be a "decision," can ultimately belong to a state or to a group of private interests. And so, to whom?

45

That's the first question. I am not sure that it can be asked or answered in this form. What remains to be invented, no doubt, is "who and what."

*Absolutely!*[6] *And yet, don't you think that it remains conceivable that a state might have a cultural politics? You had spoken, in the interview in* Passages, *of the need to develop a critical culture, a kind of education appropriate to the media, to technologies or to teletechnologies. You also speak, now, with respect to the "cultural exception," of protectionism. There can be, I think, two conceptions of protectionism. There can be a nationalist conception of protectionism, which is always dangerous for the very nation it claims to protect, since protectionism has the effect of weakening a country's technical system and system of production and, in the long run, the protectionism is bound to fail. But there can also be another conception of protectionism, which might, moreover, mobilize the concept of "différance," namely, when the protectionism is a matter of temporizing in order to come up with means of constituting an* alternative *to the schema of hegemonic development. Consequently, isn't there a need to think a cultural politics that would face, precisely, the new teletechnological horizon, which is no longer simply the horizon of the book, which has remained, until now, despite attempts of sorts to change things, the reference for cultural and educational development? Don't you think that technological evolution is itself capable of fostering alternatives to the dominant schemas of national education, as well as, in addition, alternatives to the schemas of the current culture industries, calling forth a new kind of cultural politics?*

Yes, but one must then mobilize every possible means in the service of what one wants to serve – to serve, enrich, differentiate, and not just protect in a defensive way against the processes of the homogenization of languages, of idioms, of possibilities for original invention. There is not only one way to do it, not everything is programmable. This would have to happen in effect through education, through technical training, through all of a given country's or cultural area's places of culture. All of these resources must be mobilized, but with a view to producing something that will hold up or assert itself by means other than those of state decrees or of intergovernmental agreements, within a given country or in the entire world. If one wants to protect a cultural, national, or more generally idiomatic production with the help of international treaties, there is always a risk that this will lead to protectionism's worst effects, that is to say, to the promotion or preservation of national or international mediocrity. Thus the struggle should not erect its border [*frontière*], its "front," between France and the United States, or between Europe and the United States, but *within* the United States, where the same struggle is being carried out among places, institutions, men and women who are fighting the same hegemonic, homogenizing, *homohegemonic* power. And these people in America are the allies of those who, in France or in Europe, are resisting this homohegemony. One must change the hand that has been dealt and not pose the question of the "cultural exception" in terms of intergovernmental negotiation or of economic negotiation between different industries, state-supported or not. At bottom, the question of democracy concerns, among other things, the relation between the openness of a market and public space: how to maintain the greatest possible openness of public space without letting it be dominated, I won't say by the market, but by a certain commercialist determination of the market?

I'm not able to speak about these things in the way that I would like to write about them if I had the time, sharpening the words and concepts. In order to clarify somewhat what I've just said, let's take the example you proposed, of the Grégory case and Duras's intervention. Suppose the justice system, as it is now organized, were untouchable: a popular jury, preliminary examination as it now exists – and we know what kinds of problems both the tradition of the popular jury and preliminary examination pose in this country – the prosecutor, the defense, etc. Suppose this apparatus were satisfactory – which I don't think it is. It would be a terrible thing if the march of this justice were disturbed by someone's untimely, uncontrolled, or savage interventions in the press, and if the media came as it were to interfere in the march of justice. (It is this concern that has dictated the – really very strange – rule stating that a trial cannot be filmed, for example, nor even, I think, recorded on magnetic tape. We might come back to this. It's a very serious problem.) Suppose we agreed with this statement. However, if there is a popular jury, and if its verdicts are without appeal (with certain exceptions, but we won't go into them here, despite the urgency and gravity of the problem), this means that any and every citizen must have the right to say what he or she thinks about this or that, even if he or she is wrong. Journalists who attend trials or who have information about preliminary examination have the right to make it public. Any citizen, therefore, has the right to say: "Personally, I think so-and-so is guilty or not guilty." Obviously, this right implies the duty of responsibility, that is to say, the concern to be able to calculate the effect that saying this is going to produce. A citizen must not be prohibited from speaking about a trial in process. I don't see how, in what name, you could prohibit someone from doing this.

Then comes the now well-known case of a well-known writer who, thinking she will be able to use her supposed authority without abusing it, makes a provocative declaration in the press. If her declaration was so widely reproduced, this is because, here too, the newspapers profited from it. You should not be able to prohibit the citizen in question from speaking out; no one should be prohibited from speaking out. You must simply remind her of her responsibilities, and sometimes, certainly not always, events take care of this by themselves. In this case, it didn't take long for this to happen. Very quickly it came out, and I think she acknowledged this herself, that what she had said was either irresponsible or ridiculous. But if you don't want to institute censorship everywhere, with all that it can involve of policing and other disturbing elements, you have to let her take responsibility for what she says, even if it is, precisely, careless or ridiculous. Obviously, in saying what she did, her intention was not simply to say what she believed was the truth but to serve her own image, and to say: "I have the right to say what I think about Grégory's mother and her guilt in the press because it's recognized, or because I think it should be recognized, that I have a privileged lucidity about these things, and besides, what I say is interesting," etc. It's a difficult question. Because you can't limit the right to this "speaking out" ["*prise de parole*"], with all that it implies, on the one hand, of freedom of expression and, on the other, of exploitation of the market, without risk. But you can respond by saying, and on the whole this is

48

what happened: "You are wrong," or "You are ridiculous," or "You will be a laughing-stock," or "This violence is unacceptable." Throughout what was a whole process, I have thought that, in speaking, Duras was certainly within her rights, even if it was to say what she did, even if what she said was a bunch of nonsense or a grievous sign of irresponsibility, and at the same time, I have thought that Christine Villemin and her husband have the right to protest this violent intervention of someone who was not part either of the preliminary examination or of the jury or among the lawyers who were qualified or supposedly competent in the trial. I don't see how, in what name, you could condemn either one. But this is all still going on; we are far from seeing the end of the debate. What would be illegitimate, there can be no question, would be to interrupt it.

*There has been a lot of talk about another case, the "fake interview" with Fidel Castro by the TF1 channel. This is no longer simply or strictly a matter of the market, or of the private intervention of a public persona, but concerns the responsibility of the journalist as such. A debate has opened, a suit has even been filed and, at the current stage, the French court has declared the charges brought by the plaintiff, a television viewer, to be inadmissible. Still, don't you think this raises the problem of a right and a duty of the journalist, insofar as there is a veritable . . .*

. . . now here it seems we can speak of falsification . . . The problem is different. There is what in common, everyday language would be called a "lie": falsification, false witness, or perjury. Someone presented as an interview, framed it as such, something he knew had taken place and been uttered at another time and in another setting. With reference to the most solidly accredited definition of the lie, I would say that there was a lie, not simply because someone said something that wasn't true (for it is possible to say something false or erroneous without lying), but because this someone *knew* it wasn't true and wanted to *make* people *believe* it was, because he wanted to *deceive* the addressee. In short, he sold consumers one product in another's packaging. Given the fact that there is an at least implicit contract between manufacturer, merchant, and consumer, this kind of falsification is grounds for legal action, as are any damaged or doctored goods. Once we've said this, which is hardly contestable, I think, but a bit rough, such a case of falsification can serve as an index for tracking every less spectacular mystification. Here, there is as it were a case of a blatant or quasi-blatant violation [*quasi flagrant délit*]. But wherever there is editing, cutting, recontextualization, incomplete citation in the press, on the radio or on television, there is falsification in progress. We should not try to hide this. It is what we've been talking about.

*The whole problem is in knowing what can be framed by a norm, a deontology, etc., and what can't, or how it might be possible to regulate this otherwise.*

The question of the rule or regulation has started to come back regularly here. There is no rule that could escape process: these rules change, they are flexible, they must be adapted. It's a constant struggle; we have to impose rules, but we also have to distrust them, to distrust their potential elements of censorship, inhibition, prohibition. In the case of this interview with Castro, it is clear that we have a rule at our disposition; it tells us what we are in no case permitted to do. Anyone who does this thing commits a grievous professional mistake, an identifiable violation which has justified a suit on the part of the TV Carton Jaune association.

*But the magistrates have not judged it to be justified, not yet.*

I want to interrupt this exchange for a moment to return to the question of a minute ago. If what we are in the process of recording at this very moment were to be shown live, in France, and not internationally, a certain number of viewers would doubtless be able to understand what we're talking about, that is to say, for example, the fact that, in the course of this long and drawn-out Grégory affair, a "great French writer" named Marguerite Duras said, one day, in *Libération*, that she was sure that the mother was guilty, that she knew, as always, what she was talking about, etc. But, beyond this audience, *in France, today*, no one will understand. Tomorrow, ten years from now, in France, perhaps no one will understand anything anymore. It is already enough to cross a border, to go to Spain or Italy, to say nothing of the United States or Southeast Asia, to realize that no one, or practically no one, will understand any of it. Assuming that, even in France today, our manner of speaking about all this, our rhetoric, our lexicon, the associations we're making, our way of posing certain problems or of presupposing certain shared premises did not reduce our effective audience to a very limited circle – today, and perhaps even more so tomorrow. We would have to integrate into what we're saying at this moment, if, in any case, we want the immediacy of this present moment to have some chance of being transported elsewhere, some explanatory elements that would make it possible for this interview – which would have become, in this way, a "product"– to circulate. The same goes for the allusion to the fact that Poivre d'Arvor, having presented an interview with Fidel Castro, inserted – correct me if I'm wrong – statements that Castro had made elsewhere, in another context, for other addressees, and as it were pasted them, cited them, grafted them onto his own interview, passing the whole thing off as a single exchange.[7] In this case, too, only some French viewers, who are familiar with the affair, and who are able to identify Poivre d'Arvor, will be able to understand some part of what we're saying. But for the others, we would have to insert what in a book would be a footnote in order to explain what we're talking about.

We see, here, how our present divides itself: the living present is itself divided. From now on, it bears death within itself and reinscribes in its own immediacy what ought as it were to survive it. It divides itself, in its life, between its life and its afterlife, without which there would be no image, no recording. There would be no archive without this dehiscence, without this divisibility of the living present, which bears its specter within itself. Specter, which is also to say, *phantasma*, ghost [*revenant*] or possible image of the image.

Having said this, which I hope will clarify somewhat, on the other hand, what we said a moment ago, let's go back to the case of this falsification and the rules that might as it were prohibit or punish it. You told me that, all things considered, the suit filed against the operation in which Poivre d'Arvor engaged has not been retained. Probably because he was able to persuade the judges,

alleging that he hadn't falsified anything, that he had simply presented things in such a way that, the frame having been slightly
transformed, the principal "content" of Castro's statements had
been respected.[8] This distinction between formal frame and "content" is obviously highly problematic. Crude as it may be, it is
always in effect. It has an ancient history, the entire history of law
or right, of property rights, of copyright, of author's rights (which
are another matter entirely), etc.; we should come back and treat
all these things at length. It is all too clear that this distinction has
never stood up to analysis. It is less credible than ever today, in
the cases and with the teletechnological powers we are talking
about. All artifactuality, all the manipulations we were just talking about take place through intervention at the level of what is
called framing, rhythm, borders, form, contextualization. I don't
think it would be easy to enact fixed rules, in a rigid fashion, with
respect to this.

*Don't you think the problem is ultimately on the side of the
receiver? When I spoke, in reference to the question of the "cultural
exception," of a veritable politics, I was thinking less of international treaties governing commercial trade than of a political will,
a political program that would take several specificities fully into
account: the specificity of the culture industries in their current
and future states; the specificity of the technologies they mobilize
and of their coming evolutions; and the specificity of the public
space which comes out of them today or will come out of them
tomorrow. Such a politics would make teletechnological innovation its element. And it would of necessity be constituted within
the framework of a thinking of the technical character of memory
itself and in general, within but also beyond the current era of the
industrialization of memory, which is based on teletechnologies.
To explain this hypothesis – I am thinking of the second volume
of* Memory and Rhythms, Gesture and Speech,[9] *which you yourself
cite in* Of Grammatology, *in which Leroi-Gourhan analyzes the
mass media – I have to refer, here, to the development of analog
and digital media as a process delegating scientific knowledge to
technical devices, that is to say, as an expropriation of the knowledge of individuals toward technical systems. This is the technological condition of the global symbol- and memory-production*

*industry which began after 1945, and which Marx had, moreover, already announced. It is an expropriation which forces this memory to yield to the general industrial law that imposes a division between producers on the one hand and consumers on the other. One of the major problems with teletechnologies is that they necessarily place their addressees in the position of consumer.*

*At the same time, it should be noted that current technology is, from this point of view, evolving quite a lot, particularly in the domain of image and sound treatment, and thus, of course, with the development of the Internet. New material supports are being developed in the service of what is called multimedia. Digital image technologies are generating very powerful software for the treatment and personal archiving of the image. Software which, there is some hope, will be made available to a larger public in the years to come, first in the universities and then in private homes. This software will become the "electronic larger public." It is possible to imagine that this technological evolution will profoundly modify the conditions of reception – just as, for example, rock bands have appropriated what are called "samplers" for treating the sound archive, and a new music has appeared, produced primarily through archive manipulation, which has ultimately brought a new instrumentality to these musicians and to every musical genre today. Don't you think one response to the question that is being posed under the name of the "cultural exception" would consist in taking into account the technical character of the constitution of citizenship, or in putting veritable devices of acculturation into place?*

The technical development to which you allude confirms it: not only is all regulation in the form of state law, all cultural protection decided by a nation-state dangerous in itself, but it is outdated from a technical standpoint. This has already been remarked. You will be less and less able to convince citizens that they should be content with national production once they have access to a global production from the outset by themselves. The risks of state authoritarianism are in this case doubled by its ever-increasing inefficacy. In order to respond to this, yes, programs are necessary, but here too, one must be wary of what you call "acculturation," with its potential for authoritarianism or state control. What is possible and, in my opinion, desirable are not legislative decisions concerning the production and distribution of whatever it is, but open programs of education and training in the use of this technology, these technical means. You would have to do everything possible so that, citizens or not, the users of these technical instruments might themselves participate in the production and selection of the programs in question. If you want to fight the hegemony of the "bad," "Hollywood" production, you're not going to do it by closing the market, but by promoting, through education, discussion, culture, in France and elsewhere, occasions for preferring one kind of film over another and by promoting, at the same time, a production that escapes the bad, Hollywood industry, in France *and* in America. It's a struggle for which one can elaborate new discourses – not only in a single country, but the world over, including in the United States – one can try to convince people, to ensure that the properly productive selectivity of those who were previously in the position of consumer-spectators can intervene in the market. If all these questions are concentrated around film or television today, this is because never before in the history of humanity has a form of, let's call it, in order to move quickly, techno-artistic production found itself immediately plugged into a global market of this size. A film producer knows that, if he produces this or that kind of thing, he'll be able to sell it all over the world, in thousands and thousands of theaters. Thus he can count, from the start, on an enormous budget. In truth, he would not even be able to plan and produce without this expectation [*prévision*] – or provision. Never before in the history of humanity have we seen this.

That's the critical point, and if you don't want a production that doesn't deserve it to be promoted, in the shelter of borders protected by international treaties, then you have to battle these industrial monsters with the help, one could say, of a counter-production, of another production, massive or not, and not only in France but all over the world. If this struggle were limited to France, it would be lost before it started. You've got to promote diversity of preference all over the world: preference for this film over another, possibly this American film over another, or this Hollywood film over some other Hollywood film. But if this struggle is not waged from the side of what are still called

– provisionally – the "buyers" or "consumers," it is lost from the start.

*If I have understood you correctly, the addressees must themselves participate in production.*

It is precisely the concept of the addressee that would have to be transformed. And isn't this essentially what is happening?

# 3

# ACTS OF MEMORY:
# TOPOLITICS AND
# TELETECHNOLOGY

BERNARD STIEGLER    *The technique[1] of alphabetic writing and the*
*widely shared practice it makes possible were the condition of the*
*constitution of citizenship – a distribution or sharing which has*
*grown progressively, of which Jules Ferry[2] is the modern culmina-*
*tion, but which began in ancient Greece. This technique is very*
*different from that mobilized by film and television, insofar as one*
*can't be a reader of books without in one way or another being*
*potentially a writer. It is hardly conceivable that the addressee of*
*a book could successfully read it without in some sense knowing*
*how to write. Perhaps he will never write, but he reads – it*
*becomes possible for him to read – from the moment that he*
*knows how to write. On the other hand, for reasons having*
*primarily to do with technics, film, television, and computers*
*have made it so that an addressee may have no technical com-*
*petence with respect to the genesis or production of what he*
*receives. And yet, thanks to technical evolution, machines that*
*can receive and, simultaneously, produce and manipulate are*
*becoming widely available. Hence we can imagine that practices*
*of the image will develop on the side of the addressee, in this*
*way breaking with the industrial opposition of producers and*
*consumers. There can be no doubt that this technical evolution*
*makes possible a cultural politics aimed at turning the addressee*
*into an actor or agent in production.*

JACQUES DERRIDA    The addressee has never simply been a passive receiver. If we recall, as you just have, that access to writing
in the classical sense was the condition of citizenship, this is the

very thing that is changing today. The question of democracy, such as it has been presenting itself to us here, may no longer be tied to that of citizenship. If, that is, politics is defined by citizenship, and if citizenship is defined, as up to now it has been, by inscription in a place, within a territory or within a nation whose body is rooted in a privileged territory – given, lost, or promised. All the problems we have been talking about we have been talking about with reference to a technology that *displaces places*: the border is no longer the border, images are coming and going through customs, the link between the political and the local, the *topolitical*, is as it were *dislocated*.

Anything we say in this direction must integrate a general dislocation, that is to say, the determining effect of the technologies or teletechnosciences we are talking about. A moment ago, you were saying that the addressee is actually, at least potentially, a producer, a sender, someone who must achieve mastery of the instrument. This is true, but as you also know, most of the technical devices that construct our modern space are used by people who lack the competence to do so. Most people who drive a car, who *use* a telephone, e-mail, or a fax machine, and a fortiori people who watch television, don't know *how it works*. They use these things in a position of relative incompetence. I would be tempted to see in this relative incompetence and its incommensurable increase as compared with the incompetence of the past, along with the decline of state sovereignty, one of the keys to most of the unprecedented phenomena that people are trying to assimilate to old monsters in order to conjure them away (the "return of the religious," "nationalist" archaisms[3]).

*But, that said, it is one thing not to know how something works and another thing not to know how to use it. A keyboard, piano, harpsichord, or synthesizer virtuoso may not know anything about what goes on inside the mechanism governed by the keyboard. And the piano-maker who built this keyboard is not, for all that, a musician. That's why instrumental culture cannot be reduced, as it too often is, to the culture of a technician, in the very narrow sense of the word. It is possible to know how to use something without knowing how it works. And it is possible to know how something works and not be able to use it, or to use it only very poorly.*

Yes, but what seems to be getting aggravated is the passivity with respect to this working. And so, what we have to in fact promote – we will never achieve it completely – what we have to develop is what sometimes appears under this slightly ridiculous name "interactivity": the consumer responds immediately when he is interrogated, intervening to ask his own questions, reorient the discourse, propose new rules. But all of this is done to such a feeble degree! It doesn't even come close to what we would like to see, namely, for addressees to be able to transform, in their turn, what reaches them, the "message," or to understand how it is made, and how it is produced, in order to restart the contract on different terms. Of course we're never going to achieve some kind of symmetry or reciprocity. This mirage, that the addressee might reappropriate what reaches him, is a fantasy. But this is no reason to abandon the addressee to passivity and not to militate for all forms, summary or sophisticated, of the right of response, right of selection, right of interception, right of intervention. A vast field is open here. I think, moreover, that this development will continue inexorably, at a rhythm that seems incalculable today. It's taking place, it's happening, this relative reappropriation is under way, and such a process can be seen or comes through in all of the debates or dramas we've been talking about. Above all, we should not be saying "reappropriation" here, not even relative reappropriation, but analyzing another structure of what I have proposed to call exappropriation . . .

*That there can be no reappropriation, this holds equally for print culture.*

Of course. There is no total reappropriation, but there is, by the same token, no renunciation of reappropriation either. Just because there is no possible end of reappropriation does not mean that it would be possible or desirable to give it up. This is in any case what opens the field to the desire to reappropriate *oneself*, and to the war between appropriations.

*We can imagine, precisely because total reappropriation is not possible, that a kind of knowledge might form that would intens-ify the mechanisms and the desires for reappropriation. Just as, in print culture, the school was created to develop this kind of knowledge, we can imagine that a kind of knowledge of the image might be constituted.*

If you want to pursue this comparison, we are by and large in a state of quasi-illiteracy with respect to the image. Just as literacy and mastery of language, of spoken or of written discourse, have never been universally shared (it goes almost without saying that there have always been, not only people who can read and people who can't, but among those who can, a great diversity of competencies, abilities, etc.), so today, with respect to what is happening with the image, we might say, by analogy, that the vast majority of consumers are in a state analogous to these diverse modalities of relative illiteracy.

*The analogy is really the question, for we can only talk about literacy or literacy education insofar as we're dealing with letters, that is to say, with a discrete element that the image apparently lacks.*

There do not appear to be letters, but there is certainly a montage of discrete elements. We have the impression that we are immediately overcome by a total image, impossible to analyze or break into parts. But we also know that it is nothing of the kind. It only appears this way: images can be cut, fragment of a second by fragment of a second, and this raises so many problems, especially legal problems! There is also, if not an alphabet, then at least a discrete seriality of the image or of images. We must learn, precisely, how to discriminate, compose, paste, edit.

*How would one go about developing a knowledge of the image? By making these discrete elements and their possible combinations visible, by making it possible to distinguish them?*

In saying it is imperative that we develop this critique, one does not exactly go out on a limb. It is only a preliminary condition; the experience is not exclusively critical. But the development of this critique is under way, slowly, and it can be, shall we say, if not organized and programmed by national education, then at least encouraged by every possible means, both in school and outside it. One of the problems with school is that it occupies only a limited time and space in the experience of the subject, citizen or not, who has access to the image outside school, at home, or anywhere. This critical imperative is obligatory in school and to a large extent outside it.

*It would therefore be a matter of political necessity that a new kind of relation to the image be developed, one of the conditions of which would be access established both legally and instrumentally, notably by dépôt légal and by preservation of the archive. (A condition that, with the Inathèque de France, is being put into place at this very moment.) But it would also be a matter of conceiving a politics of memory that would necessarily have an instrumental character. If we pursue the analogy with writing, doing our best to take the limits of this exercise into account, we are in fact talking about discrete regularities, that is to say, in a sense, a "grammar." Well, it is pretty obvious we can't conceive of grammarians, or therefore of teachers or of students, unless the technics of writing, which gives language this lettered relation, and the instrumental kinds of knowledge it makes possible, are to a large extent appropriated. Without this broad dissemination of a profoundly and predominantly technical-instrumental culture, it is difficult to conceive of school culture. To learn to read and write is, first of all, to learn a technique. Too often we forget this. And this technical competence is necessarily shared by "senders" and "receivers" of written texts because one has to know how to write in order to be able to read. If we take, in comparison, contemporary teletechnologies, it remains to be seen what an instrumental culture of film and television might be.*

*The question of technics therefore runs through everything we've said. In the case of the Castro "interview," the magistrates declared the charges inadmissible by arguing that the problem could essentially be ascribed to the packaging of the information, or rather to its material support, to the very nature of the support and to the fact that, in video direction, it necessarily entails editing, cutting, and so transforming and even deforming. And I understand that the magistrate did not think it within his competence to pass judgment on this point, which is irreducible in the television journalist's*

*activity no matter what. To generalize the question, shouldn't we be asking ourselves about the place of technique or technics in political and juridical thought in general? In the Western tradition, practically to this day, technique has essentially been thought under the category of the means, that is to say, as a pure instrumentality which does not in itself participate in the constitution of ends. Don't the problems we've been raising here call for a reconsideration of the question of technics? In introducing this theme, I am thinking especially of your book on Marx and all that you have developed under two words, which are the question of "inheritance," on the one hand, and the question of "spectrality" or "virtuality," on the other. Don't you think that this question of cultural politics which we've been raising is a case, one that is particularly pressing and urgent today, of the much more general question of the relationship between political community and technics? A moment ago, you said: "The link between the political and the local has been dislocated." Isn't this essentially the question of technics?*

In his arguments, the judge declared himself, at least implicitly, incompetent with respect to technical questions. Thus he presupposed that there is a gulf between juridical judgment and technics. Well, throughout history, whether it has been known or not, the judiciary has always implied a certain competence – even if only rudimentary, even if only very insufficient – as to technique, as to the difference between form and content, as to what was an instrument, what was framing, etc. And so we might actually remind juridical discourse, not simply that it implies a certain technical knowledge, even if only insufficient, but also that it is *itself* technical, even if judgment, in the purity of its decision, should in principle, and if possible, not be "technical" anymore. Juridical discourse itself includes a whole set of rules and of applications of rules, that is to say, a technology. There is a juridical technology, and no judgment, no justice is neutral or innocent with regard to technics in general.

Let's leave the example of Poivre d'Arvor aside and try to go back to the premises of your long question about a politics of memory. On the one hand, one might be tempted, in a very spontaneous way, to say: We need a politics of memory, we need to set up archives, we need to give everyone, or as many people as possible, access to the archive so that they will be able to know, work, do research. But at the same time, every politics of memory, if the word "politics" has a classical and strict sense, implies the intervention of a state. It's a state that legislates and acts with regard to the nonfinite mass of materials to be stored [à stocker], materials which must be collected, preserved, whatever the current, extraordinarily enhanced means for the storage of images may be. Today, we can at least pretend (in a dream) to archive everything, or almost everything. Not only does the Archive Nationale preserve the *dépôt légal*, the great debates, everything that constitutes national memory in the traditional sense of the term, but we can and in fact do record almost anything: the volume is enormous. But because it is not possible to preserve everything, choices, and therefore interpretations, structurations, become necessary. As soon as we speak of a "politics of memory," we may worry: Isn't it a state agency that is ultimately going to decide, when it increasingly represents this or that power in civil society, what the nation-state will have to preserve, always privileging, moreover, the national and the public? Why have we preserved what is French rather than what is German or Japanese? And what part of national history are we going to preserve?

The very fact that there is a politics of memory already poses a problem. It is necessary to have memory, we think spontaneously, and memory is better than amnesia. Suppose, for a moment, that this were unconditionally true. This memory being finite, are we going to delegate this responsibility to a so-called state institution, that is to say, to a system of powers which in fact always represents, in the name of the state – and history has taught us to think this – a fraction of the nation, if not a class, then at least something which is not the "integral will" nor often the "general will" of all the citizens of this state, citizens past, present, and future? A politics of memory is necessary, perhaps, doubtless, but it is also necessary, in the very name of this politics of memory, to educate . . . I don't dare say citizens anymore . . . I don't dare, for the same reason, say subjects either . . . it is also necessary to educate or awaken "whomever" to vigilance with regard to the politics of memory. Whoever is in a position to access this past or to use the archive should know concretely that there was *a* politics of memory, a *particular* politics, that this politics is in transformation, and that it is a *politics*. We must awaken to critical vigilance with regard to the politics of memory: we must practice a politics of memory and, simultaneously, in the same movement, a critique of the politics of memory.

*In other words, we must develop an awareness of selectivity . . .*

Yes. This awareness of selectivity will never simply be a spectatorial critique, a theoretical vigilance. We have come back, here, to the question of instrumentalization. None of this could be done without instrumentalization and without a culture of instrumentality. But at the same time – the question of language alerts us to this – there is a point at which *technique* does not mean *instrument*. "Mastery of language" does not simply signify a relation of objectivity or of objectification. There is something in memory that is neither objectifying nor objectifiable. We might say that there is always already the technical or the instrumental, and at the same time, that not every technique can be instrumentalized: critique, the "subject" of critique, will not be in a relation of pure objectivity with respect to what he treats. He will speak the language, he has to speak the language, for example, and when one speaks a language, one is not a spectator. The practitioner of language, whether it be everyday language, political language, scientific language, or poetic language, and poetic language more than any other, is not in a relation of user in the instrumental sense. There is always already technique, but this technique is not totally instrumentalizable. It is necessary – if it is necessary – to awaken to the politics of memory, to the critique of the politics of memory, but it is simultaneously necessary to awaken to the thought, and I do mean the thought, that this critique is not sufficient, if by critique one understands objectification and instrumentalization.

The "it is necessary" ["*il faut*"] we are talking about is itself not critique-able, it is not objectifiable. Why is it necessary to have memory, in the end? You are never going to prove that memory is better than nonmemory. What is more, memory includes forgetting. If there is selectivity, it is because there is forgetting. The "it is necessary" itself cannot be critical through and through, critical to the bone. Thus it is necessary to think critique. Like the politics of memory, the critique of a politics of memory calls for a thinking of what this "critical" imperative signifies. And it is necessary to try to adjust this thinking, to turn it toward the newest technical events, toward the most surprising sophistications of technics, such as they are happening or will happen to us, coming upon us from the future, from the still-to-come [*depuis l'à-venir*].

How to think, in the sense I just invoked, these technical events? How to politicize them "otherwise"? How to "democratize" them, knowing that the political may itself be the theme of this critique and of this thinking, which is not a given? It is obviously a difficult and an infinite, even an impossible task. Just now we have been accepting the need – we agree on this, I think – for a critical culture, for a politicization that would revive what is generally occulted ("depoliticized") about the political, for a sensitivity to the necessary democratization of all these phenomena. Well, at the same time, by the same token or, I would say, in the same step, we have to be wary of a certain kind of politicization, precisely insofar as the inherited concept of the political and of democracy – and it is a question of *inheritance*,[4] I'm getting to this, from Athenian democracy, along with all the revolutions that have affected the concept of democracy up to our day – insofar as this concept has been governed, controlled, and limited by the borders of the nation-state, by a territorialization, by everything we thought we understood under this fine word "citizenship," acquired or "natural," by blood or by soil. Perhaps the political must be deterritorialized; no doubt it is deterritorializing itself. Perhaps it is even necessary to think democracy beyond these "borders" of the political. We are given this imperative – to think the political beyond the political, as it were, or the democratic beyond democracy – by technics concretely, urgently, every day – both as a threat and as a chance. Every time we turn on the television or use the telephone or fax, these questions that I just raised much too rapidly, and so summarily, become unavoidable. This is not the speculative question of the philosopher who says to himself: Critique is necessary; it is necessary to go beyond critique. At every instant, the question of the border comes up. Here we are in the suburbs of Paris, and I don't have cable. When I go to Budapest, right away I can "tap in" to a much greater number of channels, I can watch CNN at five o'clock in the morning. As soon as I turn on the television, whether I'm in Ris-Orangis or in Budapest, the question of critical culture, of democracy, of the political, of deterritorialization erupts.

*All these words: citizenship, politics, border, idiom, place, territory, etc., are affected by the object of the critique we're talking about (let's call it a mnemotechnology), and by technics in general. They do not stand in a relation of exteriority to the object one would want to be able to critique in their name; they are not a secure ground from which one might designate it; they are themselves caught in the process of deconstruction and critique that this object itself demands. Do you mean to suggest, since you have spoken of your situation in relation to the CNN network when you are here, in Ris-Orangis, or in Budapest or in Paris, that "political" community – in quotes since the word "political" is itself affected by the question – would have to become something like the thinking of a community of networks, or a technological community?*

Whether one likes it or not, it is a question of a new distribution or sharing [*partage*] of these images, of this information, a sharing which is no longer governed by a territorially delimited, national

65

or regional community. I would hesitate, however, to use the word "community." I have always been resistant to this word. To speak of a "technological community" would be to risk reconstituting the very thing that is in question here. "Network" is a bit better, but it is a network without unity or homogeneity, without coherence. It is a sharing. Like Jean-Luc Nancy, I prefer the word "sharing": it both says what it is possible up to a point to have in common, and it takes dissociations, singularities, diffractions, the fact that several people or groups can, in places, cities or non-cities, as far apart as those you mentioned a moment ago, have access to the same programs – it takes all this into account. It doesn't signify a community, if by community one understands a unity of languages, of cultural, ethnic, or religious horizons. There is indeed a form of coinscription in space, or with a view to space, which doesn't correspond to the same models as before, but I would hesitate to call this a community. For all the people who have simultaneous or quasi-simultaneous access to the same sequence of information, political information for example, or to the same sequence of a presented work, this simultaneous broadcast, by cable, of the same information, of the same work, of the same film or same concert, this is certainly programmed. That it is necessary to be critical with regard to this programming does not mean that it is necessary to reject it, but that it is necessary to look with a certain eye, to interrogate, to wonder, to respond in some way. One is tempted to call a "community" all or most of the people who watch this thing at the same time, who decide or are prepared to critique it, but I would not call this a "community" because it is made from different places, with different strategies, of different languages, and respect for these singularities seems just as important to me as respect for community. In fights, in struggles, there can be solidarities, but this does not constitute a community that would establish on the European or international scale the same kind of being-together, cohesion, or obligatory solidarity as what is called a nation today. It's the schema of identity that makes me apprehensive about this word community. *There is* identification, certainly, one can neither deny nor simply fight it, but to speak exclusively in the name of the reconstitution of a simple identity which, instead of being regional or national, would become for example European or even global, this seems equally problematic and worrisome to me, politically – in the shaky sense that we gave this word a moment ago. Thus it is necessary – it is necessary, always if it is necessary – to try to train and to educate as many people as possible (I say "people," vaguely, in order to avoid determining them as subjects or as citizens), to train them to be vigilant, to respond, and on occasion to fight, but without presupposing or assigning an obligatory identification or reidentification. Disidentification, singularity, rupture with the solidity of identity, de-liaison seem just as necessary to me as the contrary. I wouldn't want to have to choose between identification and differentiation.

# 4

# INHERITANCES – AND RHYTHM

BERNARD STIEGLER   *This sharing depends, at one and the same time, on flux, on process, and on stock. It is necessary to archive and, at the same time, to be aware of the criteriology – political, economic, or other, in every possible form imaginable – that governs these stocks, to be aware that there is stock and that there is localization, including territorial localization, but this does not amount to thinking the whole problem. There is therefore a negotiation between flows, circulations in the networks, stocks that are being constituted and localized, and there has to become possible, in all of this, a sharing that would not be referred to an identity, to a stock based on identity, even if there is necessarily identification too. Under the rubric of this question – and the question of the negotiation between these poles – the theme of heritage or inheritance,[1] of what you have called "inheriting," develops.*

JACQUES DERRIDA   One does not inherit a stock, a constituted reserve that one would receive or that one would find somewhere, like a deposit. Already the schema of the stock or deposit is immobilizing, it leads us to think too quickly of localization in a place, of the sedentariness of a gross ensemble that would be collected in a single site. The archive we're talking about, or rather, the heritage, implies that a stock is never constituted, never in one piece. It is less and less localizable, paradoxically because it is always already classed, that is to say, interpreted, filtered, put in order.

Inheriting does not consist in receiving goods or capital that would be in one place, already and once and for all, localized in a bank, a data bank, an image bank, or whatever. Inheritance implies decision, responsibility, response and, consequently, critical selection, choice. There is always choice, whether one likes it or not, whether it is or isn't conscious. If heritage has never been of the order of the stock or of the reserve of an available good, well, today, given techniques of archivization, it is even less possible to speak of a stockable heritage, primarily because the sequences of inheritance can very easily be transported, dissociated, or transferred elsewhere. Just as, today, the French are no longer the only ones able to inherit the French heritage, just as the archive is no longer simply local and should no longer be simply national, so inheritance is no longer simply tied to a language, a nation, etc. The fact that we would be inheritors through and through does not mean that we are passive with respect to the past. The emphasis I've placed on this concept of inheritance does not signify a backward-looking or traditionalist approach. That we are inheritors through and through does not mean that the past dictates something to us. There is, to be sure, an injunction that comes from the past. There is no injunction that does not come from a certain past as future, as still to come [*un certain passé comme à venir*]. But this past injunction enjoins us to respond now, to choose, select, critique. Thus I would dissociate the concept of inheritance from those of patrimony, of the bank, of storage [*stockage*]. And I would say this in general and unconditionally, no doubt, but also in view of what we are talking about at the moment, namely, a certain development of the technology of the archive, of what it enjoins us to think.

*If I try to summarize what we've said, and under the heading of the question of the "cultural exception," it is too quick to oppose the national to the foreign, or democracy to the market, and the concept of the rule is too limited here. More generally, you have repeatedly used the term "process." Everything is happening as if the structures corresponding to what has up to this point been called the state – and in state there is the idea of a stability – everything is happening as if the very concept of the state no longer had the power to face a processuality in which we find ourselves caught. Don't you think that tied to this processuality is the question of the speed of the technical system's development, in*

69

*comparison with which the structures within which we have lived for centuries, for millennia even, will turn out to be structurally behind?*

There are a thousand questions here. Before going to that of process, I would like to evoke what is happening here when, instead of pursuing the necessary course or relatively interior consequence of a meditation or discussion, as we would if we weren't surrounded by this technical apparatus, all of a sudden, as if we had been interrupted, we had to start speaking in front of the camera and recording devices. A modification is produced – in any case, in me, and I don't want to pass over it in silence – which is at once psychological and affective. Another process is set into motion, if you like. I don't speak, I don't think, I don't respond in the same way anymore, at the same rhythm as when I'm alone, daydreaming or reflecting at the wheel of my car or in front of my computer or a blank page, or as when I'm with one of you, as was the case a little while ago, as will be the case again in a moment, talking about the same questions but at another rhythm, with another relation to time and to urgency. This does not mean that, at that moment, one has enough time – one never has enough time – but the relation to urgency and to rhythm would be different and now it has suddenly been transformed by this system of scenographic and technical devices. As soon as someone says "Roll tape!" a race begins, one starts not to speak, not to think in the same way anymore, almost not to think at all anymore . . . One's relation to words, to their way of coming or of not coming, is different, you know this well. The first thing to do, if what we are doing here has any specificity, would therefore be not to forget, not to subtract, not to neutralize this effect, and to record on tape, to archive the re-marking of this fact that we are recording, that I, in any case, am recording with a certain amount of difficulty. This is in general part of the experience, shall we say, of "intellectuals," of people who write or who teach, etc.: when they are in front of the camera or microphone, the more they ask themselves questions about this situation, as I am doing here, the more they exhibit reticence, scruples, a shrinking or retreat – not a gratuitous or negative retreat, but a retreat in which they try not to do just anything, to be more "responsible" – the more they are removed from this experience, the less they are accustomed to it, the less they are able to forget the artifice of the scenario. Maybe intellectuals who appear on television all the time are better able to forget the effects of this artificiality which I, for one, am having such a hard time with here. I say this under the heading of process and of stasis, of the arrest, the halt. When the process of recording begins, I am inhibited, paralyzed, arrested, I don't "get anywhere" [je "fais du sur-place"] and I don't think, I don't speak in the way I do when I'm not in this situation.

Now that I've opened this reflection or left it suspended, I'll come back to your question about process. Perhaps the emphasis I placed on this word was awkward, or the word ill-chosen. It might lead you to think – which I would not want – that what counts is becoming as opposed to structure, flux as opposed to arrested determination. No, I believe it is necessary to be attentive to processes without nevertheless neglecting discontinuities, stases, halts, structures, the heterogeneities between models, places, laws. Once we've taken this precaution, the emphasis on process should help us to see that everything we are talking about is engaged in a transformation the very rhythm of which is determining and increasingly incalculable. For it is *breaking*, it is rolling up on itself like a wave, which accumulates strength and mass as it accelerates. Even if the events that marked our generation or even the last decade with a trauma, whether fortunate or unfortunate, could be predicted, even if this or that, the fall of the Berlin wall for example, or the Rabin-Arafat handshake, or the end of apartheid in South Africa could be predicted, what was impossible to predict, even for the most discerning experts, and practically up until the eve of the event, was the instant at which it was going to happen. I think this acceleration in process is tied in an essential way and, in any case, to a large extent, to telemediatic, teletechnical transformation, to what is currently called information's voyage or route, the crossing of borders by images, models, etc. I believe that this technical transformation – of the telephone, of the fax machine, of television, e-mail and the Internet – will have done more for what is called "democratization," even in countries in the East, than all the discourses on behalf of human rights, more than all the presentations of models in whose name this democratization was able to get started. In any case, these models were

71

only able to have this effect insofar as they were suddenly crossing more quickly with images that made "the other side of the world" immediately presentable and enviable, on a television screen, in photographs, or through the discourse of journalists traveling very quickly. The acceleration by technics, and the acceleration of technics itself, the passage from radio to television, but also, within television, the multiplicity of cable networks, etc., all of this determines the starting up [*la mise en processus*] and, above all, the qualitatively heterogeneous acceleration of the process. They say that no totalitarian regime, no matter how great its political, military, or even its economic strength, can survive above a certain threshold in the density of the telephone network. Once this threshold has been crossed, police control is no longer possible, and the totalitarian straitjacket cannot hold. I took the example of the telephone, but we could take many others. The acceleration of all political or economic processes thus seems indissociable from a new temporality of technics, from another rhythmics.

# 5

# THE "CULTURAL EXCEPTION":
# THE STATES OF THE STATE,
# THE EVENT

JACQUES DERRIDA   This holds equally – I'm trying not to forget any of the points in your question – for what we have said about the "cultural exception" and for what we have said about the state. You were right to play on the word "state" with a capital S or a small s,[1] thus taking into account a *statics* that can sometimes come to prevail over this dynamics of process. When it comes to the "cultural exception," I am open to both logics simultaneously. On the one hand, I can appreciate the arguments of those who wish to resist the industrial or techno-industrial hegemony, of a certain cinema for example, insofar as it imposes, by virtue of this economic power, impoverished, homogeneous, leveling models. But then I say to myself that it may be necessary to invent means of doing this other than those of legislation. On the other hand, therefore, I am also convinced by those who propose to fight in other ways. For example, by allying themselves with those who share these views in other countries, including with those Americans who are resisting these same threats in America. Borders ought, in any case, not to be closed. On the contrary, a certain permeability ought to give debate and diversity the best chance – to give us the best chance, not for a competition, in the strictly economic sense of commercial competition, but for a veritable stimulation, for a struggle of exigencies, in "production" as well as in "reception" (to rely again, provisionally, on this pair that we had called into question a moment ago).

Between these two logics – they are equally convincing but, at the same time, competing and seemingly incompatible – is left only the very narrow pass of a negotiation without precedent

73

[*sans exemple*]. Of a negotiation whose law would have to be invented, a singular law. Each work, each event, is an attempt to "cross," without norm or general rule, such a pass . . .

BERNARD STIEGLER  *The whole question is one of negotiation.*

We've got to negotiate. We've got to understand that this crisis of the "cultural exception,"[2] such as it was both targeted and focused at a singular moment in the negotiation of GATT (General Agreement on Tariffs and Trade), was a passing moment. The question must not be closed. Whatever the decision, the question will not be settled. It will come up again tomorrow, in other terms: it, too, is caught in a process. We've got to do things in such a way that the process of upping the ante [*surenchère*] or of polemical dialogue remains open. The question of the "cultural exception" cannot be separated from the context of GATT. What it was was a moment of GATT, and GATT itself is only a moment, a very early one no doubt, in an international process that is going to last a long time.[3] The political struggle must continue.

Just as, with respect to the "cultural exception," it is difficult to give up either of the two exigencies – and it is necessary to restart the process if we don't want to be blocked, from one side or the other, by two exigencies that may become equally paralyzing as well – so, with respect to the state, it happens that I sometimes engage in a discourse with antistatist connotations, considering what the state is today, and sometimes in a statist discourse, and I don't want to give up either one. I'll explain this in a word (we can't go into it at too much length here): I'm statist when I tell myself that the state, even when it takes the form of unconditional authority or of absolute sovereignty, is a process. Despite the "eternitarian" declarations that almost always found constitutions, the state remains a moving, labile structure, the result of a relatively stabilized process. This structure nevertheless makes it possible, in a given situation, to resist certain violent appropriations. From this point of view, and to this extent, it seems to me desirable that there be a state, a state capable of checking or of regulating a certain kind of particular or private violence. In this way, it can happen that, in the country of which I'm a citizen, I would rather support the state, with all that this entails, against a number of forces or of conjunctions of interests, a number of social or economic, material or symbolic powers. But conversely, the state, today, in the form that ties it to the nation, the nation-state, represents particular interests that, once again, sometimes check an international law which is also going through, or ought to be going through, an incredibly rapid process of transformation. This law, moreover, remains a limited formation, which is often powerless compared with networks of national or international economic and teletechnoscientific powers. This point requires further explanation. I believe that the great movement in which we are engaged today, and which, ineluctably, will have to continue, is a profound transformation of international law. This law will have to reconsider the (essentially Western) concepts on which it is based today, in particular that of the nation-state's sovereignty. Today, this sovereignty seems by rights to be untouchable. It constitutes the axiom of international law. One effect of this situation is that international institutions like the United Nations and a few others have no means adequate to their mission. They are powerless, incapable of making themselves heard or understood, of laying down the law, they find themselves at the mercy of a few nation-states (we might give examples, we don't have time, but let's just say you know who comes to mind). International law doesn't exist, or at least it doesn't exist effectively to the degree it should. It is *in fact* inadequate to its own *telos*. It will no doubt always be this way. But a law that doesn't exist *effectively*, a law that is not capable of ensuring, by force – by *its* force – that its decisions are respected, is not a law or right. Kant made this very clear. Which does not mean that international institutions are to be condemned. We ought to be glad they exist, imperfect as they may be, and their perfectibility attests to their future, their still-to-come [*leur à-venir*]. Their current existence, even when it leaves something to be desired, represents an immense step forward. But at the same time, precisely, we should never forget their current inadequacy, and that this inadequacy stems especially – and doubtless, alas, will continue to do so for a long time – from the old concept of the state to which this law is currently tied, and for this same reason, from certain practices of the nation-state. Here too, there is an ongoing process, and it is not possible to think it or to think the way in which we are engaged in it, whether it be a

75

question of international law, of the state in general, of the "cultural exception," etc., without linking all these questions to certain debates around GATT, debates that are themselves indissociable from one another: debates about "labor," about the "market," about speculation and the movement of capital – and this brings me back to the heart of your question – about the accelerated development of the teletechnosciences. These are so many themes tied to what is called, in the broad sense, technics, but also to what is called, in a way that is necessary although often dogmatic and suspect, globalization.

Now, to speak of a technical process, and indeed of its acceleration, mustn't lead us to overlook the fact that this flux, even if it picks up speed, nonetheless passes through *determined* phases and structures. What bothers me about this word "process" is that it is often taken as a pretext for saying: It's a flow, a continuous development; there is *nothing but* process. No, there is not *only* process. Or at least, process always includes stases, states, halts.

*It's a matter, then, of getting to where we can negotiate with process, of negotiating possibilities for the localization of this process so that it may effectively take place. Jean Baudrillard, in* The Gulf War Did Not Take Place,[4] *formulates the problem of a not-taking-place, or of a non-place (in the process of history) – the possibility that things* don't take place *in this process, as if there were a kind of layering of events that process strips away. A moment ago, you pointed out that the development of technics was one of the essential factors, for example, in the destruction of totalitarian regimes, in "democratization." But at the same time, those who have struck gold with the theme of the "cultural exception" speak in the name of the sense, very widely shared all over the world, of a destruction, not just of totalitarianism, but of everything that seemed to constitute social cohesion in all its forms. A destruction that would be the price to be paid for the continuation of the process very widely and even principally felt, by the same token, as a threat, and as a threat to the future itself. Is it a question of inventing – with all the difficulty that consists in not being able to rely on anterior experiences which seemed eternalizable and which this process reveals are not – is it a question*

*of inventing, through negotiating, structures of localization, that
is to say: places, structures, in which something takes place? You
used the verb "to check" or "brake" ["freiner"]. You said: "It can
happen that I'm on the side of the state; I want to be on the side
of the state in order to check processes of private appropriation."
Is it sometimes necessary to put mechanisms of slowing into place
so that flux may effectively give rise to locality?*

I would never go so far as to say that we should not under any
circumstances put on the brakes. If there is negotiation, this presupposes the possibility of braking, of putting things back in gear
or restarting, and of accelerating. If something has a rhythm, this
is because speed or acceleration is not homogeneous, because there
can be deceleration. Negotiating, if one has a responsibility and if
one has decisions to make – this is pure hypothesis – may consist
in accelerating or in braking. The moment the Berlin wall was
demolished, there was a flood of immigrants or emigrants faced
with which the Western states had to put on the brakes – wrongly
or rightly, but either way, one can understand the logic of the
thing – they had to try to protect themselves against the effects of
this democratization. Wrongly or rightly, will we ever know?

Two remarks about this. First, attention to process should not
efface the event. What Baudrillard meant, I imagine, was not simply that a general process stripped all of this away, but also that,
precisely, the simulacra of images, television, the manipulation of
information, reportage had nullified the event, that in the end this
was lived only through the simulacrum. This is interesting. I
believe something like this or something analogous happened (and
no doubt always happens, has always happened, from the moment
that iterability in general structures the eventness of the event),
but this should not make us forget – and the event is unforgettable
– that there were deaths, hundreds of thousands of deaths, on one
side of the front and not the other, and that this war took place. If
this taking-place is sealed in what there is about deaths that is
ineffaceable, we should not forget that these deaths are each time,
by the hundreds of thousands, singular deaths. Each time, there
is a singularity to murder. It happens, and no process, no logic of
the simulacrum can make us forget this. For, along with process,
we must also think singularity.

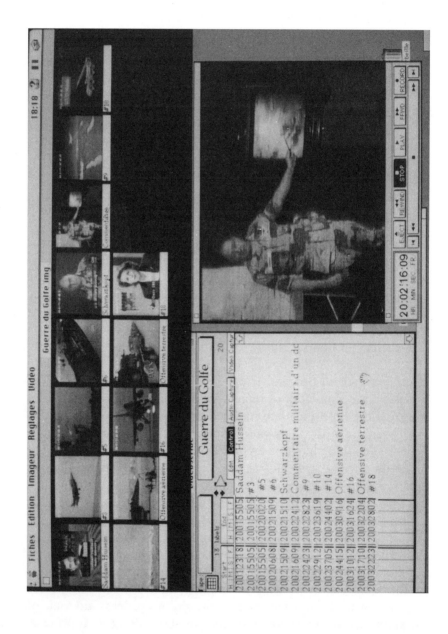

Which brings me to a second remark. If it is necessary to avoid the delusion or denegation which, in the name of technotelemediatic simulacra, would make us deny, neutralize, repress, forget the death, and the violence, and the event of the war that took place, it is also necessary to understand that it is in the name of this same singularity that people object to technics, which is always in danger, precisely, of dislodging, dislocating, exporting, expatriating singularity. Here, I will venture a hypothesis which is naturally far from an exhaustive explanation of what is happening in the world today in the form of what is currently called a "return of nationalisms," a "reappearance of fundamentalisms," twitchings around the phantasms of soil and blood, racisms, xenophobias, ethnic wars or ethnic cleansings. My hypothesis will not be adequate to everything that is going on in these things. What is going on is, moreover, each time idiomatic: each time, it's *a* nation, *a* people, *a* language, *a* minority that struggles or fights in the name of these structurally phantasmatic motives. A general hypothesis is therefore insufficient. Still, insufficient as it remains, I believe it is necessary in that it appeals to the technological process, insofar as this process also (although not only) takes the general form of expropriation, dislocation, deterritorialization. And thus also that of a decomposition or disqualification of the state as a sovereignty tied to the control of a territory. Even if this expropriation can at times produce the opposite effect (an illusion of proximity, of immediacy, of interiority), the global and dominant effect of television, the telephone, the fax machine, satellites, the accelerated circulation of images, discourse, etc., is that the *here-and-now* becomes uncertain, without guarantee: anchoredness, rootedness, the *at-home* [*le* chez-soi] are radically contested. Dislodged. This is nothing new. It has always been this way. The *at-home* has always been tormented by the other, by the guest, by the threat of expropriation. It is constituted only in this threat. But today, we are witnessing such a radical expropriation, deterritorialization, delocalization, dissociation of the political and the local, of the national, of the nation-state and the local, that the response, or rather the reaction, becomes: "I want to be *at home*, I want finally to be at home, with my own, close to my friends and family."

This is, moreover, not even a *response*, it is not a secondary reactivity that would as it were compensate or react after the fact.

No, it is the same movement. It belongs to the constitution of the proper and comes under the law of exappropriation I mentioned earlier: there is no appropriation without the possibility of expropriation, without the confirmation of this possibility.

Take the example of television. It constantly introduces the elsewhere and the global into the home. Thus I am more isolated, more privatized than ever, with the constant intrusion, desired by me, into my home, of the other, the stranger, the distant, the other tongue. I desire this intrusion and, at the same time, I shut myself in with this stranger; I want to isolate myself with him without him; I want to be at home. The more powerful and violent the technological expropriation, the delocalization, the more powerful, naturally, the recourse to the at-home, the return toward home. Once "democratization" or what we call by this name has, thanks precisely to the technologies we were just now talking about, made such "progress" (I am putting all these words in quotes), to the point where, the classical totalitarian ideologies having foundered, in particular those that were represented by the Soviet world, the neoliberal ideology of the market is no longer able to cope with its own power – once this has happened, there is a clearer field for this form of homecoming called "petty nationalism," the nationalism of minorities, regional or provincial nationalism, and for religious fundamentalism, which often goes with it and which also tries to reconstitute states. Hence the "regression" which accompanies the acceleration of the technological process, which is always also a process of delocalization – and which in truth follows it like its shadow, practically getting confused with it. Here again, because we are talking about a double or polar movement, there can be no question, it seems to me, of choosing between the two, or of saying: What matters is the acceleration of the technological process at the expense of the desire for idiom or for national singularity. Between these two poles one must find, through negotiation, a way precisely not to put the brakes on knowledge, technics, science, or research, and to accede – if possible, inasmuch as it is possible – to another experience of singularity, of idiom, one that is *other*, that is not bound up with these old phantasmatics called nationalism or with a certain nationalist relationship to language, to singularity, to territory, to blood, to the old model of the borders of a nation-state. I would like to think that the desire for singularity, and even the desire or longing for home, without which, in effect, there is no door nor any hospitality (and in any case no law and no duty of hospitality), the desire for hospitality (which exceeds both law and institution), I would like to believe that this unconditional desire, which it is impossible to renounce, which should not be renounced, is not tied in a necessary way to these schema or watchwords called nationalism, fundamentalism, or even to a *certain concept* of idiom or of language. A concept to which I would oppose another concept and another practical or even poetic experience of idiom. These motifs or these concepts, these values – of nationalism for example – have a history. They are models in which these desires for singularity have taken refuge, but they are outdated and, despite appearances, on the way to extinction today.

Perhaps it is this extinction that we would have to "negotiate," without for all that having to give up singularity, idiom, and even a certain at-home, this at-home which, I will say again, can project an image, obviously, of closedness, of selfish and impoverishing and even lethal isolation, but which is also the condition of openness, of hospitality, and of the door. I would like therefore to believe that this desire for singularity can have another relation – it is very difficult – to technics, to universality, to a certain uniformization of technics. It is in any case indissociable from it from the very first. Similarly, the relationships between different languages must not end up in absolute untranslation. Translation is necessary. One must invent an experience of translation which makes crossing possible without leveling and effacing the singularity of idiom. It is necessary to make, in translation, another experience of language, another experience of the other. Another experience of idiom, which has never been constituted or brought back to itself outside a certain experience of technics. This is what it is necessary to "negotiate" and, simultaneously, to invent. This is very difficult and it is very harrowing. The task is endless, but if there is something to "negotiate," it is this. When we say negotiation, we say compromise, transaction. Transaction is necessary, but it has to be invented . . . A good transaction is an invention as original as the most novel invention. Transaction is necessary in the name of the intractable, in the name of the unconditional, in the name of something that admits of no transaction, and that's the difficulty. The difficulty of thinking as "political" difficulty.

# 6

# THE ARCHIVE MARKET: TRUTH, TESTIMONY, EVIDENCE

BERNARD STIEGLER *In other words, it's not a question of opposing singularity to technics. They do not stand in a relation of opposition . . .*

JACQUES DERRIDA It is not an opposition, no. They are even irreducibly linked. But there is a tension between them; the tension should not be minimized.

*We could even give examples. It could be shown that writing, which is, as we have already said, a teletechnology that had destructive effects on idiomatic singularities, on forms of community, etc., at the same time that it destroyed these traditional forms, was a formidable development of singularity, of what was called, precisely, "citizenship," and of what might be called "scientificity" (there is obviously singularity in the scientific), etc.*

Of course.

*It nonetheless remains the case that the violence – of technics or of democracy itself, and which is also the violence of time, of becoming – this violence is felt very widely, including by people who aren't in the least caught up in, or who in any case don't feel caught up in nationalist or racist drives or anything of this sort. And it is felt increasingly as a violence of the market, or of a technical development dictated by a functioning of the market, a kind of blind market law. You have amply stressed that the market is not an enemy of democracy, and that it is even a condition*

82

*of democracy's development and of the singularity it makes pos-*
*sible. It nonetheless remains the case that you have also said that*
*there can be a mercantile understanding of the market, a weak*
*understanding of this market. We have talked about speed and*
*also about the relation to the future, about incalculability. The*
*market calculates. It is essentially a system of calculation, that is*
*to say, of amortization by calculation. Don't you think that,*
*indispensable as it may be to the development of democracy, the*
*market poses a problem in that it tends to be devoted to the short*
*term, subject to the demands of short-term profit?*

What is the short term today? This would be difficult to calculate,
seeing that it is impossible to determine the limits of the market
and to know what can ever escape it. I don't know that anything
ever escapes the market. What I have tried to suggest in the book on
Marx, in connection with exchange-value and use-value, is that, at
bottom, exchange-value, market value, is always already announced
in use-value, at least in the form of a haunting. Which would mean
that nothing precedes what is called the market in the broad sense.
The same difficulty presents itself again in connection with mercantilism. I used this word a bit quickly. We have certain ideas when
we say "mercantile," but to delimit mercantilist market practice,
this would be tough. Mercantilism can begin very early; it begins
immediately and does not occur above and beyond the market. And
so, what I had in mind when I used, perhaps awkwardly, this word
"mercantilism" was a practice which, paradoxically, not only because of the short term, but because it can jeopardize the market's
extension, its generalization, its enrichment, and its productivity,
risks having impoverishing effects. And this pretext of immediate
monetaristic profitability can jeopardize the very thing that constitutes the market's *chance* – in the best sense of this word.[1]

*Which is true, for example, in the domain of the publishing indus-*
*tries, of the rapid amortization not only of certain kinds of books,*
*but of certain kinds of films and of other cultural products.*

Let's try to fix the meaning of this word. If, in order to realize profit
on an investment as quickly as possible, I prefer to produce a bad
television series which will sell all over the world and, in so doing,

to jeopardize the chances of a more interesting product, in this case, mercantilism will have won out over another practice of calculation and, ultimately, over another market. Mercantilism is always relative. It is a way of privileging a certain kind of quasi-immediate profitability at any cost. The question of the immediate and of the short term is a terribly difficult one because the norms or criteria of the calculation have changed today. For example, today it is possible to do so-called basic research (gene therapy, AIDS research, etc.) which it is hoped will, twenty or thirty years from now, have beneficial effects, whereas twenty years ago, this same basic research seemed left to an incalculable future. The scale of the short and the long term gets displaced all the time, and this affects the calculability of investment in technoscientific research. Mercantilism is therefore, in the end, a very fuzzy notion – structurally vague and indeterminate in a way that stems primarily from the paradoxes in which the concepts of the market, commodity, trade, exchange-value, and by extension, money and capital are caught.

*It is also at the heart of the debate about the "cultural exception" and French film. I want to come back to this question because there is truly an expectation that this problem will be understood, not only in France but all over the world. It's an extremely important question, despite the flawed form in which it is currently being framed. Yesterday evening, I heard on the radio that the French are the most faithful moviegoers in Europe. In the debate about the accords on the "cultural exception," there are all kinds of elements of negotiation. Some of them are, shall we say, frankly flimsy, for example, the policy of quotas, protectionism in its classical form. Others are more subtle. When people say that the French state ought to be able to support its industry through subsidies in the film industry, this is something which seems to me to be of the same order as the fact that the French state has the right to develop subsidized scientific research – and it would be very difficult to see by what right you could prevent a state from developing scientific research.*

From this point of view, I would be statist, to go back to what we were saying earlier. In certain cases, independence and sovereignty of the state are a good thing.

*Consequently, it is really a question of putting the brakes on a certain process driven by what is called the short term in order to give one locality, France, in one global industrial process, cinema, enough time to change the hand that has been dealt. It is a question, not simply of resisting a process, but of transforming this process itself. The question at the heart of our entire discussion is therefore that of time. Similarly, what we were saying about new culture, education, or training is a matter for long-term policy. Would you agree that the problem with the negotiation, out of respect for singularity (which should really be, faced with amortization, of the order of the incalculable), between process and its necessary localization would be to negotiate between imperatives of the market, which, because it is necessary to amortize systems of production, are always caught up in the short term, and the maintenance of what belongs to the long term or to what is open, risky – which cannot always be a matter for private operation? In the nineteenth century, for example, the state was obliged to invest heavily in railroads, infrastructure, training, etc., before private activity could be fully developed.*

The, shall we say, categorical imperative, the unconditional duty of all negotation, would be to let the future have a future [*de laisser de l'avenir à l'avenir*], to let or make it come, or, in any case, to leave the possibility of the future open. And, to this end, to negotiate between rhythms so that, at least, this opening will not be saturated. Why did the question of the "cultural exception" become so critical? And critical first and foremost in France, for the "cultural exception" is always the "French exception"? Well, precisely because, of all the countries involved in GATT, but also of all European countries, France was, to my knowledge, the only state in which an apparatus had been put into place allowing French cinema to suffer from American hegemony a bit less than other cinemas. And to suffer a bit less from television, and also – we should never forget this enormous market, which is undergoing gigantic development – from videocassettes of films, which are being shown less than ever before in theaters and are being shown, rather, "at home." Naturally, French cinema still "suffers" from American hegemony, since it remains practically invisible or absent in the United States, especially in the original language – let's leave this question aside.

But on the whole, in terms of production, there was a slight positive effect tied to a light apparatus, invented or approved by the French state. Which made it so that, through the "cultural exception," France was able to safeguard its own exception but also to offer a model, an incentive, or an example for all countries, all cultures, which are essentially in the same situation with respect to American hegemony in film and television. It was a question of making use, as it were, of an exemplary exception in order to loosen the stranglehold of a domination and ensure that time be given time, as the expression goes, that all the chances of a certain type of invention, innovation, or as one says, creation in film not be stifled in advance, including for the Americans themselves.

*To give time time, to protect this possibility of the future, of locality, by activating the modality of localization, this is to open the possibility of inheriting.*

Yes. If the concept of inheritance has an identity (let's accept the hypothesis, but we'd have to discuss it some other time), inheriting does not simply consist in coming into possession of a common good or of a technical ability for example. One does not inherit an anonymous and universal instrument. One can come into possession of it, one can present oneself as its purchaser, one can buy it, but one cannot inherit it. Inheritance, in the classical sense, always passes from one singularity to another by way of a filiation implying language – and perhaps even the name, but in any case language – and a singular memory. Without singularity, there is no inheritance. Inheritance institutes our own singularity on the basis of an other who precedes us and whose past remains irreducible. This other, the specter of this other regards us, concerns us: not in an accessory way, but within our own identity.

From this point of view, technics[2] is, taken by itself, and all by itself, a threat to inheritance. Now, at the same time, the opposite is also true: without the possiblity of repetition, of reprise, of iterability, and therefore, without the phenomenon and the possibility

86

of technics, there would not be inheritance either. There is no inheritance without technics. Inheritance therefore stands in a relation of tension to technics. A pure technics destroys inheritance, but without technics, there is no inheritance. This is why inheritance is such a problematic and, ultimately, aporetic thing. What does one inherit? One never simply inherits an abstract and anonymous fund of capital. Suppose that one day I come into possession of an anonymous fund of capital, in some way or another, either I win the lottery or someone gives it to me without my knowing who. I wouldn't call this inheriting. In order for me to call this inheriting, it is necessary, if there is capital, that it be tied to a name, to a language, possibly to a place, which is each time singular, addressing itself to me or coming to me as a singularity, calling me to *answer* for the inheritance, that is to say, enjoining me to be responsible for what is in this way assigned to me. An inheritance is not simply a good I receive; it is an assignation of fidelity, an injunction to responsibility. Every inheritance presupposes singular marks – I don't dare say language or discourse any longer here, for reasons you already know: I don't want to exclude the possibility of an "animal" inheritance, within animal society, for example – marks without discourse, places left to a future generation, or symbolically occupied places, marked territories. Every inheritance passes by way of singular marks, but I would not necessarily say by way of discourse or by way of languages in the strict sense. These singular marks are a challenge to technics, resistances to technologization, and they are at the same time (hence the tension) appeals to technical iterability, to *tekhnē* in the broad sense, the sense from which animality would not simply be excluded.

*You referred to iterability, to repetition as the condition of inheritance, which thus negotiates perpetually with technics. A minute ago, you said that the technical apparatus being used, at this very moment, in this interview . . .*

I want to stop you for a minute. What bothers me and seems so artificial or constraining is not the fact that this apparatus is technical. Technics is everywhere, when I'm writing with a pencil or when I'm chatting around a table, or when I'm sitting at ease in front of a computer. It is this *type* of technics that I'm not used to, with its heaviness, its rigidity, this environment, this rhythm, it's this that . . .

*I understand. But this technics determines a relation to flux, to flow, to time which is completely singular, and which stems in particular from the fact that you and I are also anticipating the conditions in which what is recorded here is going to be received. For example, we are speaking while knowing intimately that the usual practice of television, and therefore of the people who are likely to watch this recording later on, consists in not stopping and in letting, as it were, the thing flow. This is very different from the practice of the book, for example, in which the book, even if it is also a process . . .*

Yes and no. Excuse me, I'm going to interrupt you again for a second. When I write, I often say to myself: "Good . . . You are paying so much attention to this sentence, you are working the breath and the syntax, you are paying attention to the rhythm, etc." And then, depending on where it is going to be read – and this is even more the case when I rework something for an interview that is going to appear in a magazine or newspaper, which does happen, even if only rarely – I know that this is going to be read very quickly; I then try to integrate into my calculation the fact that this is going to be read in this way at another speed. But this "televised" – for the televised is everywhere – is a very difficult and even impossible operation, all the more so in that there is not one reader or one readership which is homogeneous in its experience or in its culture of "reading" or "listening," "seeing," "having a look" . . .

*Right, but you are probably still anticipating that the reader of your book is not in the same position or frame of mind while reading as the reader of your newspaper article.*

Of course. Although this can happen . . .

*I think that one of the big problems posed by the media and particularly by television, which it is said is a culture of flux, stems from the fact that one actually has the feeling that it is impossible to stop.*

A certain halt, a pause of variable duration is impossible, or very unlikely, very rare . . . it's irreversible, impossible to go back or come back [*revenir*] . . .

*. . . to go back or come back, and one is consequently put in a posititition of nonreturn, even though technics is, as you just reminded us, on the contrary, iterability and the possibility of repetition. You, Maurice Blanchot, and others have analyzed this. What Blanchot called the "mechanical" [le "machinal"] was repetitiveness, which constitutes writing – and this is where we can also see the chance of idiom in technics: in this repetition, in this iterability. One could say, on the other hand, that this functioning of flux is itself governed by a certain relation to real time, to the exploitation that I'm still going to call mercantile, if I may. Everything we have said here about the great events that sent the media into crisis in a sense illustrates this dimension of things.*

Sometimes we think: One need only capture this image, and it becomes a commodity limitless in price. This stems from the redoubtable thing about these machines: by dint of extending the power of repetitions, once something has been recorded, it can be repeated an incalculable number of times. An extraordinarily extended technical reproducibility serves to mimic living flux, the irreversible, spontaneity, that which carries singularity away in the movement of existence without return. When we watch television, we have the impression that something is happening *only once*: this is not going to happen again, we think, it is "living," live, real time, whereas we also know, on the other hand, it is being produced by the strongest, the most sophisticated repetition machines.

This apparently contradictory trait distances these machines – I don't know what generic name to give them – from the book, for example, where you are of course also dealing with a certain iterability or with reproducibility, and even with the televised, but which in a sense presents itself as such, and which says to you in advance: "You can go back to the first page, or you must do it, you must reread . . ." We have, here, two experiences of repetition and of the televised that are very far apart, if not heterogeneous . . .

*We are coming back, with this, to the specificity of contemporary teletechnologies. Earlier, you insisted on the fact that the living being itself, or at least an illusion of a living present, is caught in a possibility of quasi-infinite yet finite delay. You referred to the possibility of recording the voice, the presence of the body, gesture, etc. Well, in what you just said, we see that, in another and almost opposite respect, real time nullifies delays. Everything happens as if there were both an extraordinary opening of delay – and one would tend to think that this is an extraordinary opportunity [une grande chance] – and, at the same time, a telescoping of all delay, an annulment, which gives the general sense, from which it seems to me that no one can escape, that the very possibility of reflexivity is compromised as a result. And so both these dimensions would be found in contemporary teletechnologies.*

But some people would say, contrary to what you just suggested, that the opportunity is on the other side, on the side of delay's absence. You said: "Delay is thus an opportunity." Some people think that the opportunity of television is precisely the absence of delay: one sees (one believes one sees!) live, immediately, right away, without delay, but also – or at least this is what one believes – without any intervention or without any possible manipulation. This possibility reopens the question of testimony. In a seminar I'm giving on testimony, examples of technical interventions in the judiciary apparatus of preliminary examination or testimony have often been brought up. In the Rodney King case, in California, it just so happened that a witness, equipped with a videocamera that his parents had given him, was there when police officers beat up Rodney King. Thus there was a live image of the event. The image was broadcast on all the American television stations, and this aroused the emotion you know, granting the ensuing trial a global reverberation that, under other circumstances, it would never have had. For the scene was, unfortunately, banal. Other, much worse scenes happen, alas, here and there, every day. Only there it was, this scene was filmed and shown to the entire nation. No one could look the other way, away from what had, as it were, been

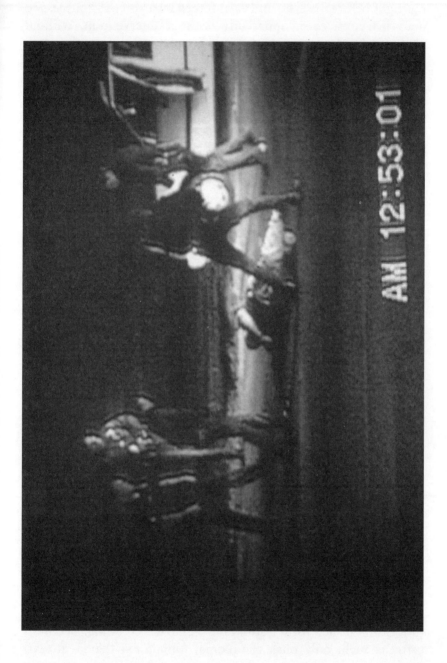

put right before his eyes, and even forced into his consciousness or onto his conscience, apparently without intervention, without mediator. And all of a sudden this became intolerable, the scene seemed unbearable, the collective or delegated responsibility proved to be too much. This did not prevent the police officers' lawyers and the prosecutor from analyzing the recorded sequence, or from trying, by breaking it into fragments, second by second, to prove the most contrary things. The one side saying: "But King tried to get up and threaten the cops, and so they were right to try to defend themselves." The other saying: "No! that's not what happened!" And in fact, the image shows, if you stop it, if you have a freeze-frame that goes to the nearest fraction of a second, that this was in no way the case, that the police had no legitimate defense. But there were still debates, extremely sophisticated analyses of the video which tried to make it say this or that. And in any case, the law did not consider this video to be a *testimony*, in the strict and traditional sense of the term. It was an exhibit to be interpreted, but the testimony could only be that of the cameraman, this young man who had the camera and who came to the witness stand, saying aloud after he had stated his name and speaking, without representative, in the first person: "I swear to tell the truth . . ." He then testified (at least, he was supposed to have) to what he in good faith thought he saw, *himself* – a camera, an impersonal technical device, being unable to serve as a witness . . .

*On the basis of this question of testimony which you just introduced, I would like to come back to the more general theme of law. Currently, although cassette tapes, sound recordings, have been mobilized in the Grégory case and the recent trial of Jean-Pierre Villemin for example, and although, when we break the speed limit, a photograph serves as evidence, our law rests on written testimony, or at least on an oral testimony and on a device . . .*

. . . It is necessary to distinguish between testimony and evidence, testimony and exhibit, testimony and clue. (Even if everything thus distinguished from testimony will have been established in its turn, as such, only on a testimonial foundation that is at least implicit and on some procedure of sworn faith. Which makes the question extremely difficult. The concept of testimony both does and does not have a limit . . . But we risk going too far afield . . . )

*. . . Our law rests on a device for the administration of evidence and on a notion of evidence which is not the same thing as testimony but which clearly affects the notion of testimony, and which presupposes this "teletechnology" that is writing. Moreover, history as a scientific practice has a lot of trouble integrating audiovisual material. Already quite some time ago, Marc Ferro argued that the audiovisual document should be recognized as a historical source, as an archive, but this approach still meets with a lot of resistance in academia, perhaps more particularly in France but not only in France. This archive definitely poses problems. Elements of what you just said about the scene of the Rodney King beating could be brought to bear on precisely these problems. To come back to real time or live transmission, Pierre Nora wrote, in 1973, in "The Return of the Event,"[3] that with the media system – he took the example of the moon-landing – the media were in a way short-circuiting historical activity and constituting the event even before the historian had the chance to do it. He described a telescoping which eliminates what he called the "work of time." Time is a kind of work. I will come back to this question in a moment, along with the work of mourning, which should be brought to bear on the question of these supports. How would you analyze the resistances, in the domain of law or of history, to the incorporation of these technical supports of testimony?*

Let's begin with a very general proposition. I shall put it in slightly dogmatic form: the entire axiomatic of law or, in any case, of the Western law we're talking about, clearly has to be and will have to be transformed and reelaborated in view of the technological mutations we're talking about. The generalization is a bit rough but, it seems to me, hardly contestable. Let's take the example of testimony and of evidence [*preuve*], which it is necessary to distinguish, which must, which should always be distinguished. A testimony has never been or should never be mistaken for evidence. Testimony, in the strict sense of the term, is advanced in the first person by someone who says, "I swear," who pledges to tell the truth, gives his word, and asks to be taken at his word in a situation where nothing has been proven – where nothing will ever be proven, for structural reasons, for reasons that are essential and not contingent. It is possible for testimony to be corroborated by evidence, but the process of evidence is absolutely heterogeneous to that of testimony, which implies faith, belief, sworn faith, the pledge to tell the truth, the "I swear to tell the truth, the whole truth, and nothing but the truth." Consequently, where there is evidence, there is not testimony. The technical archive, in principle, should never replace testimony. It may furnish exhibits or evidence, within the theoretical order that is the order of evidence, and must be foreign to the element of credit, faith, or belief implied by the testimonial pledge.

This is why I'm going to come back for a minute to the example of the Rodney King verdict: the videographic recording may have served as an archive, perhaps as an exhibit, perhaps as evidence, but it did not replace testimony. Proof or evidence – evidence! – of this fact is that the young man who shot the footage was asked to come himself and attest, swearing before the living persons who constituted the jury and who were legitimate as such, swearing that it was really he who held the camera, that he was present at the scene, that he saw what he shot, etc. There is therefore a heterogeneity of testimony to evidence and, consequently, to all technical recording. Technics will never produce a testimony. On the other hand, and we are coming back, when all is said and done, to the logic that asserted itself a moment ago – conversely, whoever testifies and takes an oath pledges, not only to tell the truth, "me, now, here, before you," but to repeat and confirm this truth right away, tomorrow, and ad infinitum. The present of my testimony must be repeated, and consequently iterability already inhabits the heart of the living present of the testimonial pledge. Testimony, as witness *borne*, as attestation, always consists in discourse. To be a witness consists in seeing, in hearing, etc., but to *bear* witness is always to speak, to engage in and uphold, to sign a discourse. It is not possible to bear witness without a discourse. Well, this discourse itself already harbors technics, even if only in the form of this iterability implied by the oath, to say nothing of this technics already constituted by the minimal grammaticality or rhetoricality which an attestation requires.

94

Hence the apparent contradiction: technics will never make a testimony, testimony is pure of any technics, and yet it is impure, and yet it already implies the appeal to technics. This contradiction or aporetic tension brings to light the necessity of rethinking the contributions of testimony and technics, and all the consequences with respect to history and to memory you've mentioned (I've tried to do this elsewhere, in a seminar, at another rhythm, in a more nuanced way, I hope, than I can do it here, improvising very quickly in front of these machines). The historian is someone who calls at one and the same time upon evidence and upon testimonies. Even if he critiques these testimonies, he implies that witnesses have declared to have done, to have seen, to have heard this or that, and he compares these testimonies to exhibits, to evidence, or to each other.

*Testimonies which, for the historian, may not be living . . .*

Yes. But what is a recorded testimony? When someone comes and swears to tell the truth, now, one time, presently, when his testimony is recorded and we have the recording of this testimony, is this recording the equivalent of testimony or not? This is the question of iterability, which I raised a moment ago. And of iterability, specifically, in "televised" form. Not only do I pledge to repeat my testimony, but my testimony may be recorded, and I accept the principle of this recording. No one testifies in secret. I testify publicly, before the jury, which represents society, etc. Thus I testify in conditions of publicity and, in so doing, I accept in advance that my testimony may be recorded, even if only by the court reporter, I accept that it may be made available and, consequently, that the recording of testimony is the equivalent of "human" and "living" testimony. Obviously, all the current possibilities of archivization, the capabilities of analog or of digital recording modify this conceptual apparatus which, in principle, must dissociate testimony from evidence.

It is an enormous history, we can't unfold it in all its complexity here because the semantic stakes are immense. In Greek, the word for testimony can also sometimes mean "evidence." It is not an accident that we have slipped from testimony to evidence. We can't embark on long analyses here for the reasons we already stated when we began. Reasons which, I would however like to underline, parenthetically, are practically "physical." A minute ago, I wanted to say that what is changing, with all these technical mutations we have been discussing, including those that constrain us, that make us uncomfortable, that oblige us to speak in a rigid and artificial way here, what is happening, and this is not accidental, is really a transformation of the body. This relation to technics is not something to which a given body must yield, adjust, etc. It is more than anything something which transforms the body. It is not the same body that moves and reacts in front of all these devices. Another body gradually invents itself, modifies itself, conducts its own subtle mutation. For example, certain "intellectuals," actors, and people who are very used to finding themselves in the situation in which we exceptionally find ourselves, you and I, now – these people have really effected a "physical" conversion which is discreet but just as astonishing, if one looks closely, as the most drastic mutations of the body. The same could be said, for us, about artificial scenes that have become routine: driving a car and working on a computer. For example, I am used to, without being used to, teaching. That is to say that, at bottom – and I try not to forget this – it is necessary to cultivate a very particular awareness in order to realize that, when you arrive in a room full of people, sit down in a chair, and start talking for two hours without being interrupted, you are playing in a very artificial theater, in which you invent yourself another body. Unless you are just leaving room for this other body, which was waiting for this all along, and which finds in all this a place of desire. Indeed, just as medical progress, the possibility of radiography, scanners, and grafts, transforms our body and our relationship to our body, media space, whether we are spectators or actors, in one way or another, implies a profound transformation of the body and of our relationship to our own body.[4]

*I suggest we come back to this question of the body and to the theme of the specter or phantom in a minute. Before we do, I would like for us to spend a bit more time on the problem of evidence. In* Camera Lucida,[5] *Barthes says that the photograph has a power of authentification. And he asserts – in a different way than does Nora, but we can compare the two – that this power short-circuits "historical mediation." I'll come back to the analyses of what he calls the "noeme of the photograph" (the "this-has-been" or "this-was" [le "ça-a-été"]), which leads him to this assertion, in a moment. But he adds that it is not a question here of exactitude but of authentification. This is with respect to the question of evidence, not only with respect to this, but it is also . . .*

Yes, he tries to prove this with respect to testimony. One has the impression, he says (although I have to admit I have some difficulty following him on this point), that the photographic effect – and I do mean the photographic *effect*, or rather the intentional noeme, the correlate of the photographic effect – consists in putting us directly, and undeniably, in front of a past that *was present*, the past such as it will itself *have been present*, so well that, all of a sudden, it has the force of authentic testimony: not of evidence, but of irrecusable testimony. Photography, as distinct from painting and literature, would have captured in itself outside itself, in the camera outside the camera, something that was there once. It is in any case thought to have, it is by virtue of its structure supposed to have, captured this irreplaceable present: *this was there only once*, and the singularity of this "only once" would be irrecusable, it would bear witness to the fact that "this was there." Not only does it prove, but it bears witness. Of course, we understand this "effect" very well, and the "poignant" emotion, to use Barthes's word, that it produces, precisely, in us. But this effect can be composed, it is not natural, it may always be artificially constructed. There is construction even in the photo that is not manipulated; and then, it can always be overwritten through all kinds of technical intervention. The extremely refined instruments of archivization we now have are double-edged: on the one hand, they can give us, more "authentically" than ever, more faithfully, the reproduction of the "present as it was"; but on the other hand, for this very reason, thanks to this same capability, they offer us more refined means of manipulating, cutting, recomposing, producing computer-generated images [*images de synthèse*], etc. The synthetic presents us, here, with a greater field and chance for authentification, and at the same time, with a greater threat to the authentification in question. This value of authenticity is both made possible by technics and threatened by it, indissociably. This is why people will continue to prefer, even if only naively, supposedly living testimony to the archive: people like to believe that, when a witness comes to the stand and speaks in his name, he is himself! He speaks . . . Even if he lies, or even if he forgets, or even if his testimony is insufficient or finite, at least it can be truthful [*véritable*]. When I pledge to speak the truth, I don't pledge to speak the true, that is to say, not to be mistaken. A witness who is mistaken does not bear false witness. I pledge not to bear false witness, to say sincerely what I saw and heard. This is the truth I pledge to tell. It is therefore something true [*une véracité*]. It is not the objective truth. A witness who comes and says, "Here's what I saw," will not be accused of perjury if he didn't see things correctly or was mistaken. He will be accused of perjury if he lies, and if, in bad faith, he doesn't say what he saw or heard, thus if he falsifies – *with a view to deceiving, with a view to making people believe* – what he knows does not correspond to what he says. False witness is not faulty witness. One will continue to have more confidence in testimony than in the archive and in evidence, while naturally neglecting all that can intervene, even in the most sincere or authentic testimony, of composition, of the unconscious, of divided personality, of schize, of all those things which ensure that the "I, here, I speak, I swear to tell the truth" presupposes an extremely complex construction.

This is all to say, in a word, much too quickly, that this mutation called psychoanalysis, which, as has often been remarked, is inseparable from a certain state of technics, has clearly not yet been integrated into law, into the concept of testimony, nor into the entire juridical axiomatic. Just as a certain thinking of the technical has not yet been integrated into law, into our law, so a certain thinking of the psychoanalytic, too, has not been assimilated, or even "included" [*"compris"*]. One might discuss *psychoanalyses*, but the psychoanalytic, that is to say, the unconscious, the taking into account of a topic of ipseity, the differentiation or the scission of agencies [*instances*], the fact that the ego is only one agency or can be a dissociated agency, all of this, with all the refinements and complications that this topic can induce, remains massively ignored by juridical discourse. Ignored in the very principle, at the very inception of law or right. Better – or worse – this discourse is built on this disavowal. Perhaps it is even instituted with a view to this disavowal.

What I am saying here is not just speculative. It has effects every day. We can't read the news or a court record without perceiving this. These effects are massive. And in the long, very long term, this situation will have to change. When it does, we will inhabit, our inheritors will inhabit a completely different world. But it's beginning, slowly . . .

# 7

# PHONOGRAPHIES: MEANING – FROM HERITAGE TO HORIZON

BERNARD STIEGLER *We were speaking, just now, of historical testimony. One whole part of the historian's work consists in reconstituting a process of testimony which is not given, for, in most of the situations in which it is done, this work can only be based on archives, on traces. Well, from one facet at least of what you've said, one might conclude that the trace cannot bear witness, and that we need the work of the historian himself, of his living testimony as it were, in order to constitute a testimony from these traces. Hence the question of photography's power of authentification can be posed a second time, in order to interrogate history as such by bringing us back, yet again, to the question of writing. There is, to be sure, no history without a certain form of writing. Many forms of writing, such as cuneiform, ideogrammatic writing, etc., can be categorized in a periodization that would put them on the side of the protohistoric. If alphabetic writing is at the heart of the historical process, both as a historical science and as a mode of life, of temporality, Geschichte, isn't this because it is a form of recording a "this-was" ["ça-a-été"]?[1] Barthes says that I cannot doubt, when I see a photographed scene, that this was (and, here, he refers to the example of a scene of bondage). Isn't this process, of the capture of a "this-was" – in another form, of course, than that which occurs with the photographic, and in a form that brings us back to everything you've said about the capture or possession of the living – already at work in alphabetic writing, and in a completely inaugural way? Isn't this writing what makes historical work possible? The work, both of the administration of evidence* and *of testimony, by which the historian is going to be able to claim – from the vantage of a certain scientific legitimacy, on the basis of technical traces – to constitute a process of testimony that is not spontaneously given in these traces, but that can nonetheless be reconstituted or synthesized?*

JACQUES DERRIDA    Just as much as evidence, testimony is *trace*, through and through. Are you referring, here, to the fact that alphabetic writing is thought to capture speech [*la voix*]?

*I would say language [*la langue*] rather than speech.*

Yes, language, but I prefer to say speech or the voice here. Language in the singular event of a phrase, that is to say, the voice. Even if it is not voiced, the possibility of the voice counts here: articulating language, pronouncing language, even if in a whisper, the voice makes language an event. It takes us from the linguistic treasure-house to the event of the phrase.

*Without the grain of the voice.*

Without the grain, yes . . . But even without utterance, language must still be tied to the possibility of enunciation – let's call this enunciation, so as to move quickly – if, at any rate, it is to produce an event. At that moment, as you see it, alphabetic writing would be tied to the event whereas another writing would not necessarily be. Not in the same way, in any case.

No doubt you are right. I have no objection to this proposition. This is what constituted this writing's progress – ultimately, what constituted this alphabetic writing itself (I would say, instead, "phonetic," the phonetic in writing) incontestably as progress, as compared with other forms of writing. This is certainly what brought it to the fore in a certain sense, and to a certain point. To a certain point, and bearing in mind the fact that not everything in alphabetic or phonetic writing is phonetic. And that which constitutes the value of the voice or, shall we say, of the event, of enunciation, is not possible by itself, without elements which alphabetic writing has in common with other forms of writing – all of this is very complicated . . . But I believe that if alphabetic writing was in a certain sense able to impose its economy in a

101

given phase of history – which I'd tried to say in *Of Grammatology* – it is because of this privilege: the alleged representation or reproducibility of the voice, of a supposedly living auto-affection . . .

*Alphabetic writing, but also photography, phonography, digital recordings, which allow synthesis, simulation, these modalities of archivization would overdetermine the possibilities for a relation to the future. If we agree that alphabetic writing brings about a new relation to the future, insofar as it opens a singular – exact – form of access to what has happened in language, to language's past, and for this reason, to the already-there – if we agree that this writing, as a new means of accessing the past, brings about a new relation to the future, then we should also say that it is a condition of the elaboration of a historical temporality. A condition, not simply of the science of the historian, but of the relation to the future constituted by historical times: a sudden acceleration, the opening of political space, the practice of geography, a transformation of the relation to territory.*

*I think we can say, in the same sense, with respect to what you have called, in* Mémoires: For Paul de Man,[2] *the "modern modalities of archivization," that these modalities are bearers of a new relation to the future insofar as they are technologies of exact recording of a new type – of a new type precisely in that they make it possible to capture* exactly *the grain of the voice, the body, and by the same token transform this very body and its psyche (we'll come back to this in a minute). We said, about the "cultural exception," that the phenomena of resistance are most likely linked to a fear for the future, for the very possibility of the future. Must this future be on the side of a new form of reflexivity? Just as alphabetic writing gave to those who lived in its space a new relation to the past, because this past became reactivatable, reiterable in a totally unprecedented form – and this is true not only for Husserl's geometrician, but for every citizen who lives in this space – aren't the current teletechnologies transforming our relationship to the past in their turn, that is to say, to the future? Writing brought new forms of reflexivity, of intelligibility, and the new relation to the future which developed in the ancient Mediterranean basin consisted both in the recording of this past and in the new forms of reflexivity it opened up. It is a very difficult*

*question, which must be asked here nonetheless: if we are record-
ing this interview before a camera and not on a paper support,
I'm assuming that this is also because we think that this is what is
called for by the reflexivity we are aiming at, a reflexivity that is
affected in its very form by its very object. Which object, at the
same time that it records our reflections about it, forces them to
yield to its own constraints. Thus the question would be that of
the relations between exactitude in its literal, in its analog, and in
its digital dimensions, and of the various relations to the future
and the reflexivity to which this leads.*

I would like to take this up backwards, so to speak. I understand
what you mean by an opening to the future that would occur in
proportion to reflexivity. Others would tell you just as readily
that reflexivity nullifies the future. Mastery by reflexivity, mastery
by reproducibility and iterability, is also mastery of a future neut-
ralized by calculation and foresight. They might say to you, in
effect, that reflexivity, and thus the technology associated with it,
closes the future off, that it anticipates to the point of mastering in
advance, by repetition, anything that might happen. It makes the
event possible, yes, but simultaneously, it amortizes it in advance.
Thus the imperative distinction is not between reflexivity and
nonreflexivity, but rather between two experiences of reflexivity,
to the extent that both are tied to technics.

And then, I am not as sure as you are that alphabetic or phonetic writing in general is privileged in its relation to the future.
I would say that all writing, even ideographic writing, supposing
that there is one and that it is pure, or pictographic writing, has a
certain relation to the future. This would be easy to show. And so,
here too, it is *modalities* of the relation to the future, to its supposed infinitude, that would have to be distinguished. All the more
in that, as you know, so-called alphabetic or phonetic writing is
not alphabetic or phonetic through and through. It always includes,
inevitably, for structural reasons, heterogeneous elements. It therefore always partakes of the forms of writing to which it is in
general opposed. Perhaps this allows us, by interrupting all the
possible developments of this too rich theme, to remark the following: teletechnological writing such as it is developing today is
anything but in the thrall of the phonetic-alphabetic model. It is

103

increasingly hieroglyphic or ideographic or pictographic as well. It is the pictogram, or in any case the pictographic effect, that television, video, cinema reintroduce.

This obliges us to complicate somewhat what we've said about the future. What is happening today is also an experience of the historical limit in its origin and in its end, in its origin and in its termination as it were, and thus, of the limit of phonetic writing. Now more than ever, the latter has been exceeded. It is not originary, in a sense it is finished, it has been exceeded by the image experiment we are conducting now. This privilege of the alphabetic, on which you rightly insist and which has struck me as well, is only a techno-economic privilege within a process that both precedes and exceeds it . . .

*But of course I didn't mean to suggest that there is no relation to the future except in the form of reflexivity that I would call historico-scientific, which is dated, remarkable for its traces. I was proposing that a certain relation to the future, which is traditionally called historico-reflexive – in the sense in which by "reflexive" one would understand "tormented by the question of rationality and of the intelligible" (in the strict sense of the word) – was overdetermined by a certain modality of archivization. And what strikes me is that this modality of archivization shares with current modalities an exactitude of recording, which elsewhere I have called the orthothetic character of these different mnemotechnics. On the other hand, if it is true that there is a congruence between the exactitude of this writing and a certain form of temporality, and if it is furthermore true that the new modalities of archivization are modalities of recording that one could say are, in a certain sense, more exact, the paradox would stem from the fact that, without meaning to privilege the Western relation to the future – which has been history as the acceleration, intensification, multiplication, and as it were expansion of the possibilities for the future – the current development of exactitude is inscribing the statement "No future" [in English in the original] all over the place. Beyond the production of this statement, which was confined, at first, to the margins of industrial communities, entire regions, entire countries, entire classes, or people excluded from any social class are saying "No future," today, in their turn.*

104

*And all those who experience political powerlessness understand this statement. In what way is the exactitude of the modern modalities of archivization capable of bringing, not a form of reflexivity that would simply be the continuation and development of the reflexivity tied to writing, but new forms of intelligibility? (It is furthermore evident, I believe I've shown this sufficiently clearly elsewhere,[3] that there is reflexivity in all technical memory, in protohistorical but also in prehistorical times.) Or, in what way, on the contrary, does this exactitude close the future off? There is, here, a problem of individual and collective intelligence about what happens and what can happen, and about the very possibility of anything happening at all.*

I don't see why you situate exactitude on the side of phonetic-alphabetic writing. It remains a question, first of all, whether it is exact, on the one hand, and it doesn't seem as exact to me as you seem to be saying. On the other hand, whatever exactitude there may be, in terms of both the concern for and the achievement of exactitude in science or in scientific rationality, it does not essentially depend on alphabetic writing. Scientific rationality has depended, on the contrary, on what, in notation, was more often than not a nonphonetic, nonalphabetic formalization. I don't deny that alphabetic writing was and remains a very useful instrument in the deployment of a certain scientificity, but the most scientific science and the most exact scientificity of science has in general been on the side of a nonphonetic and nonalphabetic formalization of notation. I would not situate all exactitude on the side of phonetic or alphabetic writing.

What is more, the impression that the horizon is closed, that there is no future, etc., may just as well be a sign of the power of archivization as the contrary. Of course, the power of or drive to archivization may open to the future, to the experience of the open horizon: anticipation of the coming event and of what one will be able to keep of it by calling it in advance. But by the same token, this increase, this intensification of anticipation may also nullify the future. This is the paradox of anticipation. Anticipation opens to the future, but at the same time, it neutralizes it. It reduces, presentifies, transforms into memory [*en mémoire*], into the future anterior and, therefore, into a memory [*en souvenir*],

that which announces tomorrow as still to come. A single movement extends the opening of the future, and by the same token, by
way of what I would call a *horizon effect*, it closes the future off,
giving us the impression that "this has already happened." I am so
ready to welcome the new, which I know I'm going to be able to
keep, capture, archive, that it's as if it had already happened and
as if nothing will ever happen again. And so the impression of
"No future" is paradoxically linked to a greater opening, to an
indetermination, to a wide-openness, even to a chaos, a chasm:
anything at all can happen, but it has happened already. It has
already happened; death has already happened. This is the experience of death. And yet, like death, the event, the other, is also
what we don't see coming, what we await without expecting and
without horizon of expectation. To be able to anticipate is to be
able to see death coming, but to see death coming is already to be
in mourning for it, already to amortize, to be able to start deaden-
ing death [*à amortir la mort*] to the point where it can't even
happen anymore. It can't even happen anymore, and everything
has happened already. This double experience, which belongs to
the structure of anticipation, to the structure of the horizon, to the
structure of mourning, too, is not new, of course. We didn't have
to wait for the machines we're talking about in order to have this
experience, but they gave it such a powerful boost that we are still
stupefied by it. We are stupefied by it on the basis of relatively
stable structures which make it so that, grosso modo, we are built
like the Greeks or like the Phoenicians or like people from the
Middle Ages, with the same existential or psychosociological structure, and yet we are not people from the Middle Ages anymore,
and suddenly, we're caught in this hiatus.

*We're behind . . .*

We're ahead and we're behind.

*There nonetheless remains the question of intelligibility. I use the
word "intelligibility" in a broad sense here. Like you, I am convinced that scientific exactitude cannot be reduced to the phonetic.
An algebraic function is represented in a graphic form which may
absolutely require phonetic writing (this is what I believe), but to*

*which phonetic writing* is insufficient, *and many mathematical notations are outside the alphabetic field. However, from a classically Husserlian point of view, which it would be very difficult to present succinctly here, the scientific gesture is itself overdetermined by a certain experience of what Husserl calls "ideality," which you have analyzed as presupposing a certain iterability, which leads you to speak of idealiterability. Well, even if alphabetic writing as such neither accounts for scientific exactitude (and I have furthermore shown that the exactitude of numeration preceded orthographic exactitude) nor exhausts its modes of notation, it nonetheless remains the case that we have difficulty conceiving of the emergence of this ideality outside a certain type of intentionality opened by writing itself, which seems to me comparable to what Barthes says about photography. If I read a dialogue by Plato, I read it while including in my intention – I'm picking up this word in the sense in which Barthes uses it – I include in my intention as a reader that this is really Plato who speaks. I deal with the thought experience of Plato himself not simply through the "intermediary" of this written transmission, but as this written transmission. Hence the significance of Husserl's text on the origin of geometry. Geometry would not be conceivable without a written mediation that not only makes it possible to reactivate geometric ideality from generation to generation, but that constitutes the possibility of this ideality as iterability. It was you, Jacques Derrida, who showed this in Husserl. But this iterability is not afforded identically by any and every kind of writing.*

*Just as Barthes can say, before the photograph, "this was," in this case too, there is a "reality effect." It is indispensable to the geometric reactivation, and it presupposes exactitude, Husserl states this very clearly. It should be added that at issue here is the exactitude of* recording. *What you just said, in pointing up the shortcomings of this Barthesian point of view, is legitimate, and doubtless Barthes himself would have agreed: the reality effect in no way guarantees the authenticity of what is captured. But it nonetheless remains the case that it elicits an* authentification effect *for the person who looks. In the same way, this effect must be at work if the reactivation of geometric intuition, of the geometrician or the protogeometrician's living present, is going to be transmitted, not simply to the next geometrician, but to the same geometrician over the course of his existence and of what Husserl calls his "flow of consciousness." There would be no idealizing reflexivity without it. Hence a certain mode of accumulation, in an "exact" form, producing a sense of exactitude and of authenticity, that is to say, of presence, would be the condition of a certain form of intelligibility. Don't you think that what we've said, on the one hand, about critical culture and, on the other hand, about the image in general is an essential part of this – the fact that the image, even if it produces an effect of continuity, is a tissue of discreteness? Isn't this discreteness, and the exactitude that corresponds to it – evident, for example, in the cinematographic reconstruction of a movement by cutting into twenty-fourths of a second – a decisive element that would effectively make it possible for us to gain a new intelligibility? Isn't it the very basis of a process of reappropriation, with respect to this advance or belatedless which "dislocates" us?*

Yes, there can be no question. This extends the field of what you call intelligibility, the field of knowledge, the field of meaning itself, but in order to accommodate the opposite effect within it: meaning and intelligibility can be extended – on the scale of what you have called the "discrete," the spacing of the discrete – only by multiplying the conditions of this very discreteness, in other words, spacing, non-sense, the blank, the interval, everything that bounds [*borde*] sense and non-sense as it were, exceeds [*déborde*] or splits it. The origin of sense makes no sense. This is not a negative or nihilistic statement. That which bears intelligibility, that which increases intelligibility, is not intelligible – by definition, by virtue of its topological structure. From this standpoint, technics is not intelligible. This does not mean that it is a source of irrationality, that it is irrational or that it is obscure. It means only that it does not belong, by definition, by virtue of its situation, to the field of what it makes possible. Hence a machine is, in essence, not intelligible. No matter what, even if it makes possible the deployment or transmission or production of meaning, in itself, as machine, it makes no sense. This absence of sense can also be dispiriting, producing effects of dehumanization, of expropriation, of nihilism. In itself, this non-sense is not an absurdity, it is not negative, but it is not positive either.

108

*It constitutes sense if it participates in its construction . . .*

Yes, but that which constitutes sense is senseless. This is a general structure. The origin of reason and of the history of reason is not rational. Whenever one says this, one is very quickly accused of irrationalism, which is stupid, even moronic. Whoever asks a question about the origin of meaning, the origin of reason, the origin of the law, the origin of humanity, and with a view to asking this particular question, must turn toward whatever bounds the very thing he is questioning: the condition of the question does not yet belong to the field of what it questions. The question does not belong to the field of the questioned. To accuse those who ask questions about man, reason, etc., of being inhuman or irrational is a reflex, even a completely primitive fright. It may be an irresistible compulsion, but it remains primitive and so testifies to this indestructible primarity. If one were to follow it out, especially in its ethicopolitical consequences, this compulsive reflex would lead to the death of the question, of science, of philosophy. And it may well be that this is the undeclared aim of this disturbing resistance. As you know, these things I'm saying are not abstract. We could give many examples of this kind of reaction, condemnation, or nervous denunciation with regard to those who ask this kind of question.

*Would you agree that meaning is constituted in a movement of reduplication [un redoublement], that it is always inscribed – and you just spoke of a technical non-sense – in a process of expropriation? We have been talking about appropriation from the start of this interview: doesn't the opportunity [la chance] lie in the capacity to tie expropriation and appropriation together by way of something that you have called "exappropriation," and that would therefore be – and this is my question – of the order of a reduplication?*

Explain what you mean by "reduplication." I'm not sure I understand exactly.

*We were saying a moment ago that it is possible to use machines without knowing how they work. But I had emphasized the fact that,* even without knowing how it works, *someone can* either know *how to use a machine* or not know *how to use it. It is possible to be an excellent pianist without knowing anything about the mechanics of the hammers that are brought into play. Conversely, it nonetheless remains the case that the pianist has an instrumental knowledge which someone who is not a pianist does not – including the instrument's maker. And it is not because pianist and nonpianist are equally ignorant of the mechanism that they are in the same situation. The "knowing" pianist has "appropriated" this kind of expropriation that constitutes the musical instrument as such, which is basically just a bunch of hammers devoid of meaning. As soon as someone stops playing it, it makes no sense. It takes on meaning only in this movement of reduplication that is usage or practice.*

I understand better what you mean by "reduplication." It is very difficult to talk about "meaning." It is, as you know, a very polysemic concept. More so than the meaning of any other word, precisely, and capitalizing this possibility, which is open for every word, the word "meaning" can always be determined differently in very different contexts, whether you oppose it to signification or to the object, whether you oppose it to what is totally meaningless, without sense (*sinnlos*, Husserl would say), whether you oppose it to what, despite the fact that it is impossible or contradictory (the squared circle for example), nonetheless makes enough sense in nonsense (*widersinnig*) to be understood as such, and rejected precisely as nonsense. There are too many folds in this concept for us to treat it seriously in the form in which we're doing this now.

Having taken these precautions, I would simply say this: there is no *meaning for* (here too, I would be careful not to determine the *who* of the *for whom*: for a subject, for a consciousness, for a man, for an animal . . . so many enormous preliminary questions), there is no *meaning for* an existence in general (and I'm not even limiting this existence to humanity or to a *Dasein*) except insofar as this process of appropriation, to use your word, is under way. This process of appropriation or of reappropriation: the one *and* (the one *as*) the other [*l'une* comme *l'autre*]. In order for "this" to make sense, I must be able, for example, to reduplicate, to repeat, even if only virtually, I must be able by virtue of this iterability to appropriate: to see what I see, to get closer, to begin to identify, to recognize, in the broadest sense of these terms – these are all processes of appropriation in the broadest sense. There is meaning only on this condition. But by the same token, there is meaning only insofar as this process of appropriation is, in advance, held in check or threatened by failure, virtually forbidden, limited, finite: meaning does not depend on me, it is what I will never be able to reappropriate totally. And what I call "exappropriation" is this double movement in which I head toward meaning while trying to appropriate it, but while knowing at the same time that it remains – and while desiring, whether I realize it or not, that it remain – foreign, transcendent, other, that it stay where there is alterity. If I could reappropriate meaning totally, exhaustively, and without remainder, there would be no meaning. If I absolutely don't want to appropriate it, there is no meaning either. And so what is necessary (the "failing" or "lack" of this "it is necessary" [le "faillir" de ce "il faut"] is existence itself in general) is a movement of *finite appropriation, an exappropriation.* "It is necessary" that I want the thing to be mine, and this holds as much for love relationships as for eating and drinking, perception and mourning. It is necessary that I try to make the thing mine but that it remain other enough that I have some interest in making it mine, other enough that I desire it. Intentionality is a process of appropriation by repetition, by identification, by idealization: I appropriate the other or an object or whatever. And first and foremost "myself," the "I" itself which must also be appropriated by an appropriating-appropriated *ipse,* whose "power" (marked in what binds *ipse* to *potis,* then to the *hospes* and to the *hostis* of *hospitality*) does not yet have the form of egohood, much less that of consciousness. But at the same time, it is necessary that what I appropriate remain outside, that it remain sufficiently other or different (from me) to still make sense. There is mourning on all sides. The condition of sense, in general, is a finite appropriation, an exappropriation. For an infinite being, there is no meaning. For a being who can't appropriate anything or who can appropriate everything, nothing makes sense. The condition of sense is the tension of this law, the double law (*double bind* [in English in the original], if you like) of the most general law on the basis of which we are able to "approach" meaning, existence, intentionality, desire. This approach can only distance . . .

*It is also the condition of inheritance.*

Heritage or inheritance is what I can't appropriate, it is that which accrues to me and for which I am responsible, which has fallen to me as my lot, but over which I have no absolute right. I inherit something that I must also transmit: shocking or not, there is no right of property over inheritance. That's the paradox. I am always the tenant of an inheritance. Its trustee, its witness, or its relay . . . I can't appropriate any heritage without remainder. Beginning with language . . .

*What you say very much reminds me of what Heidegger's* Being and Time *calls "being-for-death," even if it cannot be reduced to it.*

Many of us have consecrated analyses to this theme, and I give up in advance on trying to recall them, however briefly, in this kind of interview. I'd rather not even begin to talk about it, it is so complicated and serious, it implies so many histories, concepts, and texts. I won't say that it would be unamenable to television in general, but if you want us to talk seriously about being-for-death with reference to this text by Heidegger, I want twenty hours of television. And for those who would watch those twenty hours of television to have already read certain things. Only then will we be able to say something that "means" something, that has a little necessity or pertinence. Otherwise, there's no point in even trying. I have to say, not against television, but against the state of television today, that it is not possible to discuss a text like *Being and Time*, for example, on television. I take this example, but the same could be said of so many other things it is impossible to talk about on television in a penetrating or pertinent way! This does not mean that we have to give up on ever doing it, but – and this is happening slowly, little by little we are doing it – that we have to change television, that we have to change all these spaces and times. Perhaps someday we will be able to do much better. I hope so.

# 8

# SPECTROGRAPHIES

BERNARD STIEGLER   *I would like nonetheless to come back to the question of death, with or without direct or explicit reference to* Being and Time *– let's at least say that it would be necessary in certain respects to go there – insofar as, in Barthes, the analysis of photographic intentionality is inscribed in the question of narcissism and of mourning. Narcissism would be radically affected by the photographic experience in its strictly technical dimension. We have talked a lot about Barthes, whom I would like to cite so that I may then cite you, not from a book, but from a film in which you played yourself –* Ghostdance[1] *– and in which you say a number of things about film and ghosts. There is a thematic of the ghost and of the specter which is at the very heart of your book on Marx, but which has been insistent in your work for a very long time, which incessantly comes back there. Barthes writes, in* Camera Lucida: *"I call 'photographic referent,' not the optionally real thing to which an image or sign refers, but the necessarily real thing that was placed before the lens, without which there would be no photograph. Painting, on the other hand, can feign reality without having seen it." He adds, a bit further on: "[I]n photography, I can never deny that the thing was there. Past and reality are superimposed. . . . The photo is literally an emanation of the referent. From a real body which was there proceed radiations that come to touch me, I who am here. The duration of the transmission doesn't matter. The photo of the departed being comes to touch me like the delayed rays of a star. A kind of umbilical cord ties the body of the photographic thing to my gaze: light, though impalpable, is really a carnal medium here, a skin*

113

"He is dead and he is going to die."

*that I share with the one who was photographed. . . . The bygone thing has really touched, with its immediate radiations (its luminances), the surface that is in turn touched by my gaze.*"[2]

*Commenting on these lines, you have written that "the modern possibility of the photograph joins, in a single system, death and the referent."[3] Already in this commentary, you spoke of the "phantomatic effect," which Barthes himself had put forth.[4] In the film, in which you play yourself, you say to Pascale Ogier, your partner: "To be haunted by a ghost is to remember what one has never lived in the present, to remember what, in essence, has never had the form of presence. Film is a 'phantomachia.' Let the ghosts come back. Film plus psychoanalysis equals a science of ghosts. Modern technology, contrary to appearances, although it is scientific, increases tenfold the power of ghosts. The future belongs to ghosts." Might you elaborate on this statement: "The future belongs to ghosts"?*

JACQUES DERRIDA   When Barthes grants such importance to touch in the photographic experience, it is insofar as the very thing one is deprived of, as much in spectrality as in the gaze which looks at images or watches film and television, is indeed tactile sensitivity. The desire to touch, the tactile effect or affect, is violently summoned by its very frustration, summoned to come back [*appelé à revenir*], like a ghost [*un revenant*], in the places haunted by its absence. In the series of more or less equivalent words that accurately designate haunting, *specter*, as distinct from *ghost* [revenant], speaks of the spectacle. The specter is first and foremost something visible. It is of the visible, but of the invisible visible, it is the visibility of a body which is not present in flesh and blood. It resists the intuition to which it presents itself, it is not *tangible*. *Phantom* preserves the same reference to *phainesthai*, to appearing for vision, to the brightness of day, to phenomenality. And what happens with spectrality, with phantomality – and not necessarily with coming-back [*revenance*] – is that something becomes almost visible which is visible only insofar as it is not visible in flesh and blood. It is a night visibility. As soon as there is a technology of the image, visibility brings night. It incarnates in a night body, it radiates a night light. At this moment, in this room, night is falling over us. Even if it weren't falling, we are already in night,

as soon as we are captured by optical instruments which don't even need the light of day. We are already specters of a "televised." In the nocturnal space in which this image of us, this picture we are in the process of having "taken," is described, it is already night. Furthermore, because we know that, once it has been taken, captured, this image will be reproducible in our absence, because we know this *already*, we are already haunted by this future, which brings our death. Our disappearance is already here. We are already transfixed by a disappearance [*une disparition*] which promises and conceals in advance another magic "apparition," a ghostly "re-apparition" which is in truth properly *miraculous*, something to see, as admirable as it is incredible [*incroyable*], believable [*croyable*] only by the grace of an act of faith. Faith which is summoned by technics itself, by our relation of essential incompetence to technical operation. (For even if we know how something works, our knowledge is incommensurable with the immediate perception that attunes us to technical efficacy, to the fact that "it works": we see that "it works," but even if we *know* this, we don't *see* how "it works"; seeing and knowing are incommensurable here.) And this is what makes our experience so strange. We are spectralized by the shot, captured or possessed by spectrality in advance.

What has, dare I say, constantly haunted me in this logic of the specter is that it regularly exceeds all the oppositions between visible and invisible, sensible and insensible. A specter is both visible and invisible, both phenomenal and nonphenomenal: a trace that marks the present with its absence in advance. The spectral logic is de facto a deconstructive logic. It is in the element of haunting that deconstruction finds the place most hospitable to it, at the heart of the living present, in the quickest heartbeat of the philosophical. Like the work of mourning, in a sense, which produces spectrality, and like *all* work produces spectrality.

To come back to the *Ghostdance* experience, I regret the expression that came to me while improvising (the scene you cited was improvised) from start to finish. I remember it from this one sentence because it was a rather singular experience with Ken McMullen, the English filmmaker: we had studied that morning, in the bar of the Select, for an hour, a scene which lasted a minute, and which we repeated, repeated, repeated to the point of

exhaustion. Then, that afternoon, in my office, conversely, we improvised from beginning to end a completely different scene, it was very long, which Ken McMullen kept almost in its entirety and in which the exchange you mentioned was shot. Thus I improvised this sentence, "Psychoanalysis plus film equals . . . a science of ghosts." Of course, upon reflection, beyond the improvisation, I'm not sure I'd keep the word "science"; for at the same time, there is something which, as soon as one is dealing with ghosts, exceeds, if not scientificity in general, at least what, for a very long time, has modeled scientificity on the real, the objective, which is not or should not be, precisely, phantomatic. It is in the name of the scientificity of science that one conjures ghosts or condemns obscurantism, spiritualism, in short, everything that has to do with haunting and with specters. There would be much to say about this.

With regard to emanations and the very beautiful text by Barthes which you cited, rather than problematize what he says, I would like to tell you what happened with this film, *Ghostdance*. Having invented this scene with Pascale Ogier, who was sitting across from me, in my office, and who had taught me, in the intervals

between shots, what in cinematic terms is called the *eye-line* [in English in the original], that is to say, the fact of looking eye to eye (we spent long minutes, if not hours, at the request of the filmmaker, looking into one another's eyes, which is an experience of strange and unreal intensity: you can imagine what this experience of the eye-line can be when it is prolonged and passionately repeated between two actors, even if it is only fictional and "professional"), and after she had taught me that, then, after I had said roughly what you repeated, I had to ask her: "And what about you, do you believe in ghosts?" This is the only thing the filmmaker dictated to me. At the end of my improvisation, I was to say to her: "And what about you, do you believe in ghosts?" And, repeating it over and over, at least thirty times, at the request of the filmmaker, she says this little sentence: "Yes, now I do, yes." And so, already during shooting, she repeated this sentence at least thirty times. Already this was a little strange, a little spectral, out of sync, outside itself; this was happening

119

several times in one. But imagine the experience I had when, two or three years later, after Pascale Ogier had died, I watched the film again in the United States, at the request of students who wanted to discuss it with me. Suddenly I saw Pascale's face, which I knew was a dead woman's face, come onto the screen. She answered my question: "Do you believe in ghosts?" Practically looking me in the eye, she said to me again, on the big screen: "Yes, now I do, yes." Which now? Years later in Texas. I had the unnerving sense of the return of her specter, the specter of her specter coming back to say to me – to me here, now: "Now . . . now . . . now, that is to say, in this dark room on another continent, in another world, here, now, yes, believe me, I believe in ghosts."

But at the same time, I know that the first time Pascale said this, already, when she repeated this in my office, already, this spectrality was at work. It was already there, she was already saying this, and she knew, just as we know, that even if she hadn't died in the interval, one day, it would be a dead woman who said, "I am dead," or "I am dead, I know what I'm talking about from where I am, and I'm watching you," and this gaze remained dissymmetrical, exchanged beyond all possible exchange, eye-line without eye-line, the eye-line of a gaze that fixes and looks for the other, its other, its counterpart [vis-à-vis], the other gaze met, in an infinite night.

You will remember what Gradiva said: "For a long time now, I have been used to being dead."

This is what I meant to say a moment ago when I spoke of inheritance. In inheritance, there is always this experience which I dubbed, in the book on Marx, the "visor effect": the ghost looks at or watches us, the ghost concerns us.[5] The specter is not simply someone we see coming back, it is someone by whom we feel ourselves watched, observed, surveyed, as if by the law: we are "before the law," without any possible symmetry, without reciprocity, insofar as the other is watching only us, concerns only us, we who are observing it (in the same way that one observes and respects the law) without even being able to meet its gaze. Hence the dissymmetry and, consequently, the heteronomic figure of the law. The wholly other – and the dead person is the wholly other – watches me, concerns me, and concerns or watches me while addressing to me, without however answering me, a prayer or an

injunction, an infinite demand, which becomes the law for me: it concerns me, it regards me, it addresses itself only to me at the same time that it exceeds me infinitely and universally, without my being able to exchange a glance with him or with her.

"The visor effect" in *Hamlet*, or what in any case I have called this, is that, up or down, the king's helmet, Hamlet's father's helmet, reminds us that his gaze can see without being seen. There is a moment where Hamlet is very anxious to know whether the witnesses who saw his father, Marcellus and Horatio, saw his eyes. Was his visor up? The answer is: "Yes, he wore his visor up," but it doesn't matter, he could have worn it down: the fact that there is a visor symbolizes the situation in which I can't see who is looking at me, I can't meet the gaze of the other, whereas I am in his sight. The specter is not simply this visible invisible that I can see, it is someone who watches or concerns me without any possible reciprocity, and who therefore makes the law when I am blind, blind by situation. The specter enjoys the right of absolute inspection. He is the right of inspection itself.

121

And this is why I am an inheritor: the other comes *before* me,[6] I who am before him, I who am because of him, owing to him [*l'autre est* avant *moi devant moi qui suis devant lui*], owing him obedience [*lui devant obéissance*], incapable of exchanging with him (not even a glance). The father comes before me, I who am "owing" or indebted [*avant moi qui suis "devant" ou redevable*]. The one who watches or concerns me is or comes before me. The predecessor has come before me [*est arrivé là avant moi devant moi*], I who am before him, I who am because of him, owing to him [*qui suis devant lui*], owing him everything [*lui devant tout*]. This is the law of the genealogy of the law, the irreducible difference of generation. From the moment that I cannot exchange or meet a glance, I am dealing with the other, who comes before me; an absolute autonomy is already no longer possible. And I cannot settle my debt, I can neither give back nor exchange because of this absence of the other, which I can't look in the eye. Even if I do it or think I do it, viewer and visible can only succeed one another, alternate, not be confused in the other's eye. I can't see the eye of the other as viewing and visible at the same time.

This is why I am in heteronomy. This does not mean that I am not free; on the contrary, it is a *condition of freedom*, so to speak: my freedom springs from the condition of this responsibility which is born of heteronomy in the eyes of the other, in the other's sight. This gaze is spectrality itself.

One has a tendency to treat what we've been talking about here under the names of image, teletechnology, television screen, archive, as if all these things were on display: a collection of objects, things we see, spectacles in front of us, devices we might use, much as we might use a "teleprompter" we had ourselves pre-written or prescribed. But wherever there are these specters, we are being watched, we sense or think we are being watched. This dissymmetry complicates everything. The law, the injunction, the order, the performative wins out over the theoretical, the constative, knowledge, calculation, and the programmable.

It is in this way that I would be tempted to understand what Barthes calls "emanation." This flow of light which captures or possesses me, invests me, invades me, or envelops me is not a ray of light, but the source of a possible view: from the point of view

122

of the other. If the "reality effect" is ineluctable, it is not simply because there is something real that is undecomposable, or not synthesizable, some "thing" that was there. It is because there is something other that watches or concerns me. This Thing is the other insofar as it was already there – before me – ahead of me, beating me to it, I who am before it, I who am because of it, owing to it [*avant moi, devant moi, me devançant, moi qui suis devant lui*]. My law. I have an even greater sense of the "real" when what is photographed is a face or a gaze, although in some ways a mountain can be at least as "real." The "reality effect" stems here from the irreducible alterity of another origin of the world. It is another origin of the world. What I call the gaze here, the gaze of the other, is not simply another machine for the perception of images. It is another world, another source of phenomenality, another degree zero of appearing.

*A singularity.*

Yes, and it is not simply a *point* of singularity. It is a singularity on the basis of which a world is opened. The other, who is dead, was someone for whom a world, that is to say, a possible infinity or a possible indefinity of experiences was open. It is an opening. Finite-infinite, infinitely finite. Pascale Ogier saw, she will have seen, she did see. There was a world for her. From this other origin, this one that I cannot reappropriate, from this infinitely other place, I am watched. Still, today, this thing looks at me and concerns me and asks me to respond or to be responsible. The word "real," in this context, signifies the irreducible singularity of the other insofar as she opens a world, and insofar as there will have always been a world for her.

To link this statement up with that of spectrality, let's say that our relation to another origin of the world or to another gaze, to the gaze of the other, implies a kind of spectrality. Respect for the alterity of the other dictates respect for the ghost [*le revenant*] and, therefore, for the non-living, for what it's possible is not alive. Not dead, but not living. This is where I try to begin in the book on "Marx's specters," when I ask myself how to "learn how to live" and what "learning how to live" might mean. There is no respect and, therefore, no justice possible without this relation of fidelity or of promise, as it were, to what is no longer living or not living yet, to what is not simply present. There would be no urgent demand for justice, or for responsibility, without this spectral oath. And there would be no oath, period. Someone pointed out to me that the word "specter" is the perfect anagram of "respect." I since discovered by chance that another word is also the perfect anagram of these two, which is "scepter." These three words, respect, specter, and scepter, form a configuration about which there would be much to say, but which goes without saying, too. Respect would be due the law of the other, who appears without appearing and watches or concerns me as a specter, but why would this unconditional authority, which commands duty without duty, without debt, even beyond the categorical imperative, still be figured by the spectral phallus of the king, by the paternal scepter, by an attribute which we would have to obey just as we would the finger and the eye? The scepter would be to the finger what the phallus is to the penis. Would its fetishistic spectrality be enough to unsettle the identity of the sex organ, the virility of the father? These are questions. In any case, for it is the case, as it happens, here is a very lucky thing: these three words are composed of the same letters. This chance can only arise, don't you think, thanks to alphabetic writing – and in a singular language.

*Barthes mentions touch, you recalled this a moment ago. He certainly had a number of reasons for doing so, but it was probably first and foremost in order to insist on the technical character of this effect. He analyzes the way photography functions in its mechanical, chemical, and optical dimensions.*

We have the impression, and it would be difficult to avoid this feeling, that a substitution can be made for all the senses except touch. What I see can be replaced. What I touch cannot, or in any case, we have the feeling, illusory or not, that touch guarantees irreplaceability: hence the thing itself in its uniqueness.

*Barthes says that in order for the reality effect to take place when I see a photograph, it is actually necessary – if for example I am looking at a portrait of Baudelaire, photographed by Nadar – it is actually necessary for the rays emitted by Baudelaire's face as photographed by Nadar to have touched a photographic plate, for this plate to have been duplicated, and consequently, for luminances to have touched all the duplicates, and that there be a properly "material" chain ensuring that, ultimately, these luminous emanations will end up touching my eye, and so there is, in all this, a . . .*

. . . a series of contiguities . . .

. . . *of* material *contiguities, contiguities on the order of matter, which effectively ensures that this thing is looking at me, it is watching me, it concerns me, and it touches me, but I cannot touch Baudelaire's face. It touches me, but I can't touch it, and there is, with what Barthes calls the* spectrum *(the photograph itself), this "visor effect" and spectrality in the sense you just described. I want to emphasize matter and technicity. Barthes's sudden and rather striking interest in technicity leads him to say that a camera is a "seeing clock," a magnificent expression. I emphasize this now because you mobilize this thematic in your* Specters of Marx *(the subtitle of which we should also remember:* The State of the Debt, the Work of Mourning and the New International*), which you moreover announced in a way, without having planned it, at the time of* Ghostdance, *since you say: "It would be necessary to work through this question starting with Freud and Marx." That was over ten years ago. I am talking about matter here especially because everyone knows that Marx is the theorist of dialectical materialism and because you end up challenging Marx's philosophy as a definite figure of materialism – while at the same time doing justice to a certain materialism – on the basis of this question of the specter. You do this by showing the degree to which this question is at work in Marx, the degree to which it is thematized throughout his entire oeuvre, and to which it unsettles it and frightens him, by showing how he criticizes this mobilization of the specter in Stirner and how, at the same time, he is himself haunted by this question. And this leads you to disturb, on the basis of what you call a "hauntology," the distinction that Marx is able to make between exchange-value and use-value. It also brings us back to the questions we were just discussing*

125

*with respect to the market. Doesn't the Marxian thought of justice stumble here, in the face of a structural difficulty that would essentially have to do with technics? Again, technics is at the heart of all this, and with it and its spectrality, time – it is not possible to dissociate, in this distinction, technics and time.*

On this point, as on many others, Marx's thought – I don't dare say Marx's philosophy – this thought which divides itself into a philosophy and something other than a philosophy, seems to me tormented by contradictory movements. Which, incidentally, obey a common law. On the one hand, no doubt better than anyone of his time, Marx understood, let's call it, so as to move quickly, the essence of technics or, in any case, the irreducibility of the technical, in science, in language, in politics, and even the irreducibility of the media. He paid constant, obsessive attention to the press, to the modern press, to what was developing between the press and politics at the time. Few thinkers of his time sharpened their analysis of the political stakes of the effects of the press to this degree. On the other hand, as you just reminded us, he paid attention, in a way that was almost compulsive, to the effects of spectrality – I have tried to show this in as precise a way as I could. But at the same time, he shares with all philosophers and perhaps with all scientists . . . dare I call it a belief? in any case, the axiom, at once naive and sensible, according to which there is no such thing, the phantom does not exist. It must not exist, *therefore* we have to get rid of it, *therefore* we have to be done with it. Here you have a "therefore" that would already be enough to rattle good sense from the inside. For if there is no such thing, why would we have to chase after the specter, to chase it out or hunt it down? Why would we have to let the dead bury their dead, as Marx says in the *Eighteenth Brumaire*, in the biblical tradition? Why would we have to analyze phantomality to the point of making it disappear? Marx reproached Stirner for not doing it properly, and he had, in his critique of Stirner, compelling arguments – we would have to look at it closely – for indicating the conditions on which phantomality could be critiqued, just as fetishism can be critiqued, to the point of making them *effectively disappear* (the question of fetishism, like that of ideology, is at the center of this debate about spectrality). All of this proceeds from a point where Marx

126

reminds us that the ultimate foundation remains *living* experience, *living* production, which must efface every trace of spectrality. In the final analysis, one must refer to a zone where spectrality is nothing. This is why Marx seemed to me to contradict or to limit the movement that ought to have prompted him to take technicity, iterability, everything that makes spectrality irreducible, more seriously. And even the motif of justice – I don't dare say eschatology – a certain "messianicity," which is in my opinion irreducible (I am not talking about messianism), a messianicity irreducible in its revolutionary movement, ought to have made him more respectful of the spectral. (I try elsewhere to show why. I am not able to do it here.) He didn't make this gesture, he *couldn't* make it, he *had to not* make it; I don't know how or in what modalities to present this kind of necessity. But in any case, there is a classical movement in his text to deny all spectrality a scientific, philosophical, political, or technical dignity, or in any case a dignity of thinking or of the question, etc., and this seems to me to constitute an essential limitation of his work, its rootedness in a metaphysics of the effectivity of the living present . . .

*As regards the 1848 Revolution, he demonstrates that a return of the dead tormented this revolution, like that of 1789, but he criticizes this revolution insofar as it didn't know how to bury its dead.*

One would have to analyze closely this movement and this text of the *Eighteenth Brumaire*. In it, Marx consecrates admirable analyses to the return of the specters that made the revolutionary discourse, and even the revolutions, possible. There's a moment where he announces that the coming revolution, the social revolution, the one that failed in 1789 and in 1848, the coming revolution as social revolution, will have to put an end to this separation between form and content, to the inadequation between what he calls the "phrase" and the "content," and so will put an end to this need for dressing up in specters' clothing, in the costume of the past or of phantomatic mythologies, in order to bring the revolution off. What he announces is the end of specters. He announces that the ghost of communism, which, according to the *Manifesto*, was haunting the European powers, this ghost will have to become, through the revolution, fully present, and so cease

127

to be a ghost, and that this is what the powers of the old Europe, including the papacy, are as it were afraid of. For once the *social* revolution has taken place and this ghost of communism has *presented* itself, and presented itself in person, at this moment, for this very reason, there won't be any ghosts anymore. And so he believes in the disappearance of the phantom, in the disappearance of the dead.

This statement seems very grave to me. In its implications and in its consequences. That is why, even if I have saluted Marx in this book, what I say on this subject may be taken for a fundamental reticence with respect to what he said, and with respect to the politics and even to the idea of justice that this discourse carries within itself. As soon as one calls for the disappearance of ghosts, one deprives oneself of the very thing that constitutes the revolutionary movement itself, that is to say, the appeal to justice, what I call "messianicity" – which is a ghostly business, which must carry beyond the synchrony of living presents . . . But I am not able to show this here . . . I must refer you to *Specters of Marx . . .*

*History itself is an effect of spectrality. The return of the Romans in the French Revolution would belong to a mode of spectral transmission which overdetermines all historical events, and this in an irreducible way. Perhaps one should say, furthermore, that this spectrality belongs to what could be called a history in deferred time, a history in the play of writing, which has the structure, it seems to me, with the exception of a few very particular cases (such as signatures on contracts or events of the clearly performative type), of an irreducible distension between the event and its recording. It seems to me that, in an essential way, orthographic writing constitutes a deferred time. Today, we are living a number of events "live," "in real time." To what extent – this is yet another extremely complicated question – is the spectrality at work in this kind of transmission incommensurable with this spectrality in deferred time? In other words, what is the problematic of event-ization [événementialisation] that is taking shape around this today?*

In principle, every event is experienced or lived, as one says and as one believes, in "real time." What we are living "in real time," and what we find remarkable, is access precisely to what we are not living: we are "there" where we are not, in real time, through images or through technical relation. There happen to us, in real time, events that aren't happening to us, that is to say, that we aren't experiencing immediately around us. We are there, in real time, where bombs are exploding in Kuwait or in Iraq. We record and believe that we are perceiving in an immediate mode events at which we are not present. But the recording of an event, from the moment that there is a technical interposition, is always deferred, that is to say that this "différance" is inscribed in the very heart of supposed synchrony, in the living present. Past events, for example a sequence in Roman history such as it is mimicked, reconstituted in simulacrum during the 1789 Revolution, are clearly something else, but something else which tells us that what happened there, in Rome, is the object of new recordings. We record again, this happens to us again, and through historical reading, historical interpretation, even through mimicry, the mimetic, or simulation, we record what is past. The imprint, in essence, continues to be printed. The shortening of the intervals is only a shrinking in the space of this "différance" and of this temporality. As soon as we are able – this is an effect of modernity, an effect of the twentieth century – to see spectacles or hear voices that were recorded at the beginning of the century, the experience we have of them today is a form of presentification, which, although it was impossible and even unthinkable before, is nonetheless inscribed in the possibility of this delay or of this interval which ensures that there is historical experience in general, memory in general. Which means that there is never an absolutely real time. What we call real time, and it is easy to understand how it can be opposed to deferred time in everyday language, is in fact never pure. What we call real time is simply an extremely reduced "différance," but there is no purely real time because temporalization itself is structured by a play of retention or of protention and, consequently, of traces: the condition of possibility of the living, absolutely real present is already memory, anticipation, in other words, a play of traces. The real-time effect is itself a particular effect of "différance." This should not lead us to efface or minimize the extraordinary gulf separating what today we call real-time transmission from what had been impossible

129

before. I do not want to try to reduce all of technical modernity to a condition of possibility that it shares with much more ancient times. However, if we are going to understand the originality and the specificity of this technical modernity, we must not forget that there is no such thing as purely real time, that this does not exist in a full and pure state. Only on this condition will we understand how technics alone can bring about the real-time "effect." Otherwise we wouldn't talk about real time. We don't talk about real time when we have the impression that there are no technical instruments.

*It is also an opportunity [une chance], if what a moment ago I was calling reflexivity can only be conceived in deferral. And what you've just said calls into question the opposition, set forth by Paul Virilio and to which many people are referring at the moment, between television and text [l'écran et l'écrit].*

These oppositions remain very useful and even productive, but even as one uses them and puts them to work, one has to be aware of their limitations. Their pertinence is restricted.

*Everything we are saying about spectrality is tied to the question of inheritance – they are in fact the same question – which is very important in the thematic you are developing at the moment, and very important in the quotidian reality we are living. It is at the very core of Heideggerian thought, in* Being and Time, *particularly in paragraph 6, in which he writes – and this brings us back to a spectrological or "hauntological" analysis: "The past does not follow* Dasein *but has rather always already preceded it."[7] A structure of coming-back [revenance] constitutes* Dasein. *And in some ways, one could say that Heidegger, well beyond* Being and Time, *is one big spectrological analysis.*

Yes . . . I'd like to say something about this in a minute, yes . . .

*This being the case, one could also venture a critique of Heidegger for the same reasons, and for reasons related to the critique you make of Marx, insofar as, even if Heidegger, undoubtedly, has opened this question to a much larger extent by inscribing the*

130

*irreducibility of coming-back at the very core of his thought –*
*since it is nothing other than temporalization – it nonetheless seems*
*he is seeking, not to purify the event (what he calls "resolution")*
*of all spectrality (he shows that every event is rooted in this kind*
*of spectrality), but to purify this spectrality of its technicity.*

As you know, the thought of technics in Heidegger is at least
double; it resists any univocal simplification. Before coming back
to this, I would like to highlight a difficulty. Doubtless Heidegger
places this dimension of inheritance at the heart of existence, and
so at the heart of the existential analytic of *Dasein* – and the
theme appears very early, to be developed especially at the end
of *Being and Time*. Doubtless the concept of *Unheimlichkeit*, of
"uncanniness" – which may well define, in Heidegger as in Freud,
the element of haunting (the other at home, the reapparition of
specters, etc.) – is at the center of *Being and Time*. This could be
shown, but it hasn't been much remarked or analyzed until now.
And yet, despite this, Heidegger almost never speaks, it seems, of
the phantom itself, of the ghost [*le revenant*] itself, as if he were
wary of what this concept naturally implies of obscurantism, of
spiritualism, of dubious credulity. As I have noted elsewhere,[8] the
word "phantom" appears only once, if I am not mistaken, in a
rather rhetorical form, in an argument about time and about that
which, in time, might seem not to be. This rhetoric moreover
confirms this wariness with respect to the very word phantom and
to the credulity that goes along with this indistinct mirage. So, in
a way, at the very moment where, in his analysis of temporality or
of inheritance, he insists, as you pointed out, on what ought to
open the field of a kind of spectrology, he guards against the
spectral. One might say that, when he speaks of *Geist* (I've tried
to show this elsewhere), the specter (which also means *Geist*) is
never far off, and that, in texts such as those devoted to Trakl in
*On the Way to Language*,[9] the phantom is there. And yet, he
doesn't talk about it, he doesn't make it a theme, as we are trying
to do right now. What particularly interests me in what he says
about inheritance is notably the structure he designates by citing
a phrase from Hölderlin. For Hölderlin, we are inheritors in our
very being: language is as it were given to existence, to *Dasein*, to
man as *Dasein*, so that he will be able to bear witness, not to this

or that thing, but to bear witness to the fact that he is an inheritor in his very being. We inherit language in order to be able to bear witness to the fact that we are inheritors. That is to say, we inherit the possibility of inheriting. The fact that we inherit is not an attribute or an accident; it is our essence, and this essence, we inherit. We inherit the possibility of bearing witness to the fact that we inherit, and this is language. We receive as our share the possibility of sharing, and this is none other than the possibility of inheriting. This structure seems circular, clearly it is, but it becomes all the more striking as a result. We are drawn into this circle in advance. We inherit nothing, except the ability to inherit and to speak, to enter into a relation with a language, with a law, or with "something" that makes it possible for us to inherit, and by the same token, to bear witness to this fact by inheriting . . . We are witnesses, by bearing witness to – and thus by inheriting – the possibility of bearing witness.

*And the impossibility of inheriting too.*

As well as the impossibility of the task of inheriting which is left to our responsibility. It is in this space, this home outside itself, that the specter comes. There is nothing; we inherit nothing. In fact, the dead are dead. And, as Marx reminds us by citing the Gospel, we let, we can always want to let the dead bury their dead. But this in no way changes the law of the return – I mean, here, of the return of the dead. Just because the dead no longer exist does not mean that we are done with specters. On the contrary. Mourning and haunting are unleashed at this moment. They are unleashed before death itself, out of the mere possibility of death, that is to say, of the trace, which comes into being as immediate sur-vival – and as "televised."

And then, the fact that there is no such thing, that this doesn't exist, in no way absolves us of the task. On the contrary, it assigns an infinite responsibility. Autonomy (we are left alone with duty and the law) as heteronomy (which has come from the place of the death of the other, as death and as other); the injunction can no longer be reappropriated. The law and mourning have the same birthplace, that is to say, death. It is always easy and tempting to abuse this by saying that something can be reduced

132

to "nothing." And in effect, this objection and this abuse may always leave us without any response. This possibility (of abuse or of the "no response") is irreducible, it *must* remain irreducible, like the very *possibility* of evil, if responsibility is going to be possible and significant, along with decision, ethics, justice, etc.

Let's come back to the most difficult part of your question. Heidegger, a thinker who is very attentive to the great question of *tekhnē*, to the question of the relation between technics and philosophy, technics and metaphysics, technics and the West, perhaps remains, at a certain moment, tempted by a certain relegation of the technical to a secondary position in relation to a pretechnical originariness or a *physis*. Naturally, this *physis* is not what will later and in everyday usage be called "nature," but insofar as it *is*, insofar as it is being itself or the totality of being, *physis* would not yet be, or not in itself, *tekhnē*. Here, a presence, a present, or a presentifiable essence, a being as presence of *physis*, would perhaps reconstitute itself, not simply before any technics in the modern sense, but before any *tekhnē*. Even if *tekhnē* belongs to the movement of truth, there would be, in *physis*, something like a truth that would not be *tekhnē*. I am only marking out here, in the conditional, a big problem in the reading of Heidegger who, on this point as on others, cannot be reduced to the simplicity of this or that proposition. But how can we overlook a Heideggerian "pathos" which, despite so many denials on this subject, remains antitechnological, originaristic, even ecologistic?

*Earthy [Terrien].*

Earthy. But we also have to take into account the distinction, so insistent in Heidegger, between the "earth" and the "world." Still, even if we neutralize this "pathos" and these connotations, even if we confine ourselves to Heidegger's least ambiguous statements (when he reminds us that, in his eyes, technics is not evil, as he is often made to say), it remains the case that he tries to think a thought of technics that would not be technical (the thinking or essence of technicity is not a technicality). Isn't he tempted to subtract, in this way, the thinkable or thinking from the field of technics? Doesn't he suggest that there is a thinking pure of all technics? And in his eyes, that techni*city* is not technical, that the

133

thinking of technics is not technical, this is the condition of thinking. He would not say that the thinking of essence is neither thinking nor essence. This gesture by which he incessantly reminds us that the scientificity of science is not scientific, this gesture in which one hopes to think [*pense penser*][10] the ontological difference, that is to say, the fact that the essence of this is not this, and that this is the condition of thinking, ensures that between thinking and technics, as between thinking and science, there is the abyss of which Heidegger wants to remind us. This is, for me in any case and if I understand it correctly, the title of an immense question – and of an immense reserve with respect to the ensemble not only of what Heidegger thinks, but of what he thinks of thinking in general. Even if I find it necessary or important not to reduce thinking to philosophy, or to science, or to technics, it seems to me that to try to make of thinking or of the thinkable something that is pure of all philosophical, scientific, or technical contamination (I don't confuse these three domains, but it is a question of determinations that stand in the same relationship here), it seems to me that this purification of the thinkable is not self-evident. Nor is the desire for purification in general, the desire for the safe and sound, for the intact or immune (*heilige*), the pure, purified, or purifying restraint (*Verhaltenheit*), this theme that is so insistent in the *Beiträge* . . .

# 9

# VIGILANCES OF THE UNCONSCIOUS

BERNARD STIEGLER  *Apropos of the desire for purification, the worst collective phantasms it can engender, and memory, you recently said something approaching the following: "Every country has its original history and its economy of memory. In France, a particularly opaque, resistant, and dangerous accumulation and stratification of silence are at work, a pact of secrecy. If the breaking of the seal now under way is slow, discontinuous, and contradictory in its effects as in its motivation, this is because of the ghost. One ghost recalls another. Even as we remember the worst out of respect for memory, for the truth, for the victims, the worst threatens to return. The two memories bolster, aggravate, and conjure one another; they are, necessarily, again and again, at war, always on the brink of every possible kind of contamination." In this interview which you granted to* Passages, *you answered a question about a call to vigilance which, you said, you recently felt it was your duty to sign. Might you continue here, pursuant to what we discussed earlier, with what you were thinking at that time?*

JACQUES DERRIDA  It is a question of the vigilance of memory itself. In proportion as one remembers, as one opens the archives, as one reactualizes, in order to guard against the worst, in order to condemn or conjure the worst, the worst comes back or threatens to come back, it is called back or remembered. Vigilance, then, is increasingly necessary, and it is necessary for the conscious, "cultivated" citizen, for the "decision-maker." But, at the same time, one must know that this vigilance, this language of

135

vigilance, which is the language of consciousness or of conscience, is not enough. Nor is educating the decision-makers. The text you just cited points to a labor that clears a path and makes its way through the individual or national unconscious. A "psychoanalytic"-type labor is urgently necessary, one that could not be reduced to discourse or to an awakening. Awakening is necessary; it is necessary to work, to work to say, to see, to remember thematically, consciously, but while knowing that another analytic labor is under way. This must be done according to procedures which are no longer those of vigilance in the usual modalities of lucid waking and of the conscious ego. The citizen, in the present form of citizenship, in his current situation, must doubtless be vigilant: this is what we do, for example, when we take a position, engage in a discourse, act in order to convince, in order to exert pressure, in order to bear witness, when we go out into the streets, vote, or sign a text. This exercise of vigilance is indispensable, but we mustn't think that it's enough to become conscious, to say or see things clearly, that this is what it takes for this work to get done. This work is a labor which comes through the unconscious, through relations between forces, a scene of work that, if scene means visibility, is not even a scene anymore. It is going on somewhere else, at rhythms we can't control, in relation to which we aren't obliged to be passive, but which imply, despite everything, at the very height of our activity, a kind of passivity. This is taking place, it is happening. Moving very quickly and putting it as simply as possible, this means – without leaving any excuse for abdications, cowardice, or passivity on the part of citizens – that, despite everything, the activity of discourse, awakening, the "taking of positions," or what is called political action, all of this takes up only limited space in this work of the "unconscious," of the, shall we say, national, political, collective "unconscious," for which perhaps even the currently accredited categories of psychoanalysis are not yet sufficient. Not even the category of the unconscious, first of all. It is necessary not simply to work while simultaneously taking psychoanalysis into account, but to put psychoanalysis to work just as we have inherited it, precisely, just as we are inheriting it, if it's going to be a match for the things we're talking about here. Perhaps it is necessary to *mobilize* psychoanalysis. We just spoke of this necessary mobilization from the point of view of a reelaboration of the law, of civil law, of penal law, of international law. It is also necessary to mobilize psychoanalysis with respect to the questions we've been discussing: the work of mourning, collective memory, political ghosts [*revenants*], the "televised," spectral traces of all kinds. To work, through psychoanalysis, within psychoanalysis, or to put psychoanalysis to work: this is at one and the same time a task, a situation, and a process that is under way . . .

*In the same interview, you said that Hegel was right to remind the philosopher of his time to read the papers daily. "Today, the same responsibility obliges the philosopher to learn how the dailies, the weeklies, the television news programs are* made, *and by whom. He must ask to see things from the other side, as much from the side of the press agencies as from that of the teleprompter, etc." Might you tell us about your practice – everyday and scholarly, or somewhere in between – with regard to the press and the media?*

I'll give you an improvised and naive response, for the little time we have left: I watch a lot of television, both because it fascinates me – a fascination which I can't even pretend to justify as fascination – but also because I try, at the same time, to analyse this fascination and to know what is going on on the other side. Similarly, when I read the papers, more and more I am teaching myself to understand what might be going on in production: who decides, who chooses what, who selects what, what happens to a television news presenter, with the teleprompter for example. In this story of gazes we were just talking about, what happens to the visor effect on television? What is its future? (For we are only at the beginning of this story of televisual or multidimensional media.) I give myself the alibi of this analysis to appease my conscience with regard to this fascination and the time it makes me waste. I spend much too much time, I think, watching television, and I reproach myself at the same time, naturally, for not reading enough anymore or for not doing other things. And I also think, at the same time, of the time this makes so many others waste or save. From now on, there is this whole other economy of our time! In order to justify myself in this regard, I tell myself that it is indispensable. It is a political task, in particular, simply to watch

television, because of the effects it engenders on the political scene, but also because I should understand how this is done or made, how it is fabricated, who has the power, who chooses, what are the relations of forces, etc.

*And what kind of programs do you watch, aside from the news?*

Oh! All kinds of things, the best and the worst. Sometimes I watch bad soap operas, French or American, or programs that give me a greater cultural awareness, such as those on the Arte channel, political debates, spectacular political encounters in general, *L'heure de vérité*, *7 sur 7*, or else old movies. I could spend twenty-four hours a day watching good political archives . . . And so I watch a little of everything. It depends a lot on what time it is. What few people I know watch regularly, I suspect, and I watch very regularly Sunday morning, from 8:45 to 9:30, are the Muslim and Jewish religious programs, which I find very interesting – and if we had time to talk about them, I'd tell you why. Sunday morning, I almost never miss these two programs when I'm home. Then comes the Christian hour: Orthodox, Protestant, then Catholic. You've got to ask yourself why, for that matter, they show the Muslim program earlier in the morning. And why the Muslim religion, which is, after the Christian religions, the most widely represented in France, is the one that is "broadcast" at the worst hour, on the assumption, perhaps, that Muslims get up earlier, should get up earlier . . . You catch my drift. Afterwards, it's the Jewish program. That said, the content of these programs, for those who would analyze it, is interesting, from a properly religious as well as from a social and cultural point of view. The Muslim program includes a religious part and a social part, and I try to imagine what is going on with the producers of this program in France, their politics – there would be much to say about this, we don't have the time. In general, it is extremely smart, but in the end it translates a politics, and I find this interesting. It's the same with the Jewish program, which occasionally (it is inconsistent) teaches me a lot about the texts and the religion, but also about the ideological strategy or the political "positions" of those who are responsible for these programs, whether they are declared openly or not.

*Throughout the course of this interview, we have spoken of the need for inventing a new relation to television, and you just now said that you regularly watch the Arte channel. Can you tell us how you understand its difference, so to speak, and how it contributes to a positive evolution in the field of invention?*

First, whatever Arte's future, however much it could be transformed or improved, we should remember once again that all of this is caught up in a process. Arte is not perfect, and I am sure its directors know this. But I will say flat out that Arte is a good thing, a good invention, and that we should do everything to ensure that this invention will not be threatened. If it is fragile, I think we should mobilize to get rid of these threats. What makes it such a good invention? However inchoate it may be, it is first of all its relative independence with respect to the market, about which we have spoken a great deal, and the fact that it is at least bilingual or bicultural.[1] Which is, if not a great first, then at least,

with this kind of continuity and this kind of organization, something very new and something that takes us in the direction
of what we just said about translation, about the multiplicity of
idioms which do not exclude one another, which are not effaced
in homogenizing translation. All of this is very good. It is so good
that it ought to be developed, and it ought to be developed beyond the Franco-German duel, and even within this duel and this
hegemony, it ought to be diversified still further. And then, there
is this argument which was taken seriously during the debates
about this channel or about other, analogous inventions, the argument according to which the more one specializes a channel in
nonprofit cultural or educational programming, in something that
is more or less "difficult" – and let's not exaggerate, Arte is not
the most difficult thing we might imagine for television! – the
more one specializes this field of culture and of difficulty, the
more one impoverishes other channels and gives them an excuse
for not giving any space to culture or to education anymore.
To these things that one often dares to describe as "boring" or
too "intellectual"! This alibi argument is not entirely without
value, but on the whole, it is not convincing. As for the difficulty
argument, this is the newspapers', television's, and radio's big
problem. There is no fated difficulty. Difficulty does not exist in
itself, in the state of nature. Difficulty is something which is often
imagined or projected by this or that side, and often by certain
journalists (only by certain ones). They believe that the threshold
of readability or of intelligibility is not where they themselves are
able to understand, but where they imagine that the Audimatized
"people" understands, which prohibits or limits any pedagogy,
this intelligent and inventive pedagogy which ought to be an
essential duty of the media in general, a pedagogy which educates
for difficulty and which educates or forms the addressee. Without
constraint, without inculcation, without coercion, the media ought
to participate as much in a formation as in an information of the
addressee, who can moreover often "spontaneously" have access
to things that are much more difficult than one might think. Thus
the difficulty argument deserves separate treatment – and a good
deal of suspicion when it is used by this or that side.

And then, contrary to what these people say, the fact that there
is more culture and more things that are, say, less facile on Arte,

far from serving as an alibi for the other channels, inscribes them, if Arte is doing its job, in a competition, an upping of the ante, a stimulation that ought to incite everyone to do – and to make people want – more and better, and thus to enrich themselves with "culture" and things that are "difficult," to use these two words which in this case I find a bit silly. Therefore I am, like many people, very much in favor of the existence and development of this channel, and even of the multiplication of inventions of this kind. It is in this space, whether we call it Arte or something else, that the "televisual" presence and intervention of intellectuals and writers can take place. Those who, among the "intellectuals," feel a certain reticence, not with respect to television in general, but with respect to the current state of frames, rhythms, norms, have got to want to see this state audaciously transformed. You've got to make things that seem impossible possible. You've got to try doing things that risk extravagant failure. In order to take these risks, you obviously have to have money. You have to tell yourself that your ratings may drop. If you don't risk abrupt drops in the ratings, if you don't give yourself time for these experimental drops, you are never going to get the chance to change anything interesting on television. Arte is at least a space in which you are liberated, to a certain extent in any case, from the *immediate* control of the ratings such as they now exist. They are trying to change the ratings, and to make it so that, *in the future*, there will be more and more people who are interested in Arte and, consequently, who will stimulate or challenge the logic of other channels. I say bravo to Arte so wholeheartedly that I want to see other, similar inventions.

*As we have said, the* dépôt légal *of radio and television makes it possible for historians and other researchers specialized in this area to have access to a sizeable share of archives. This is very significant for historical science and for the sciences of the image and of sound, present and future. And yet there remains the following problem: if it is true that a science exists only by virtue of its capacities for publication, if science is, in an essential way, a modality of the transmission of knowledge, currently, rights to the image, property rights, copyright or author's rights, etc., still pose an obstacle to researchers' ability to mobilize the images themselves in their research work, to inscribe them within this research work, in its material form, that is to say, in its final form, whether we're talking about a dissertation, a book, an article, etc. In other words, there is a kind of structural interdiction, for example for the historian, against including specifics of the media he studies in historical material as such. This is all the more paradoxical in that technology is at the moment evolving very quickly in a direction which is in fact already making possible an evolution toward new material supports of knowledge – from a technical if not from a commercial, economic, legal, and cultural standpoint. What do you think about this situation?*

Well, to give a somewhat telegraphic response, let's say that, naturally, this mutation in the supports, in the very concept of the support, is going to happen anyway, at one rhythm or another. It is a question of speed and of time. There will come a time when, in effect, one will be able to and will have to integrate images into the presentation of knowledge. I don't know to what point this is impossible today, but in any case, it is still very limited. My only reticence here would be motivated by the fact that, sometimes, one may be tempted to utilize images in the presentation of knowledge to the detriment of the rigor of anterior knowledge, and this can be very dangerous. But as long as the incorporation of these other supports, of these images, of these new types of archives in a dissertation, in a book, or in the presentation of knowledge would not be made to the detriment of requirements to which one must continue to hold, I do not see any reason for trying to stop it. I have sometimes been given films in the place of written work from American students in my seminar in California. Two of them sent me films that they had made in response to what I was asking. Respecting the theme of the seminar, they were to propose a text from a corpus of their choosing, in the usual paper form. These two had sent me videocassettes which they had produced and edited in an otherwise clear enough relation to the problematic of the seminar. And so it was not inappropriate. My impulse was to accept this innovation, although it was at the time not commonly allowed in this milieu. I did not accept them, however, because I had the impression, in reading or in watching their production, that what I was expecting from a discourse, from a theoretical elaboration, had suffered from this passage to the image. I did not refuse the image because it was the image, but because it had rather clumsily taken the place of what I think could have and should have been elaborated more precisely with discourse or writing. It was a difficult negotiation. I didn't want to seem reactionary and backward-looking by saying to them: "No, you have to send me this on paper," but at the same time, I didn't want to yield on seemingly more traditional requirements, to which I continue to hold. And so I wrote them a letter telling them, in substance, this: "OK. I am not opposed to this in principle, but there has got to be as much demonstrative, theoretical power, etc., in your videocassette as there would be in a good paper. Once you have done this, we can talk about it."

*There does not yet exist a scholarly (if not scientific) practice of the image, nor a practice of the image that would be widespread in academia, but this will have to come.*

It ought to be encouraged, but provided that we don't pay too dearly for it, provided that rigor, differentiation, refinement do not suffer as a result – the rigor, differentiation, refinement which our heritage continues to associate with the classical form of discourse, and especially with written discourse, without images and on a paper support.

*The new supports are already multimedia. Already, there is not just the book or the image or sound anymore, but all these things on a single support: the compact disc, the multimedia CD-ROM.*

That's what I told them, in a slightly cruder way, when I said: "Had your film accompanied – or been articulated with – a discourse refined according to the norms that matter to me, I'd have been more receptive, but this was not the case, what you are proposing is coming *in the place of* discourse, but it does not adequately *replace* it."

# The Discrete Image

*Bernard Stiegler*

For Julien

This text was first published by the École des Beaux-Arts d'Aix-en-Provence in the collection *Art/Photographie numérique. L'lmage réinventée* (Aix-en-Provence: Cyprès, 1995). It comes out of two lectures, the first of which was given at Aix, at the invitation of Louis Bec, and the second at the Institut International de la Marionnette de Charleville-Mézières, at the invitation of Sally Jane Norman.

*The image in general* does not exist. What is called the mental image and what I shall call the image-object (which is always inscribed in a *history*, and in a *technical* history) are two faces of a single phenomenon. They can no more be separated than the signified and the signifier which defined, in the past, the two faces of the linguistic sign.

The critique proposed by Jacques Derrida of the *opposition* of these two concepts (in the sense in which the signifier would be a *contingent variation* of an *ideal invariant*, which would be the signified) is definitive. Just as there is no "transcendental signified," there is no mental image in general, no "transcendental imagery" that would precede the image-object. (There does remain the question of transcendental *imagination*, which I won't go into here.)

If there is clearly a *difference* between mental image and image-object which is nevertheless not an opposition, this means that they always have something to do with one another, that neither can make the other's difference disappear.

The difference which asserts itself most immediately is that the objective lasts, whereas the mental is ephemeral. Similarly, a souvenir-object lasts (the kind you buy at a souvenir stand, write in a datebook or diary, tie in your handkerchief – and it can last a very long time, for millions of years, if a relic is really a kind of objective souvenir), whereas a "mental" souvenir is ineluctably effaced – and in no time: living memory, lived memory is essentially what gives out; it always ends up releasing us. Death is nothing other than a total effacement of memory. It is said of an old African man who is dying that he is a burning library – except that (as compared with the old African man) the burning of a library (which is in itself a souvenir-object) is an accident: *in principle*, the library lasts. Whereas, *in principle*, death is inscribed in life itself (this is why the old man is old), as its "normal" or "natural" term, so to speak.[1]

If without the mental image, there is not, has never been, and will never be an image-object (the image is only an image insofar as it is seen), *reciprocally*, without the objective image, despite what one might think, there is not, has never been and will never be a mental image: the mental image is always the *return* of some image-object, its *remanence* – both as retinal persistence and as the hallucinatory haunting or coming-back [*revenance*] of the phantasm – an effect of its permanence. Or again: there is neither image nor imagination without memory, nor any memory that would be originarily objective. The question of the image is therefore also and indissolubly that of the trace and of inscription: a question of writing in the broad sense. I'm going to try to show this so that I will then be able to specify what is happening *today* to the objective image, *that is to say*, to the mental image.

In the history of the image-object, the great event specific to the nineteenth century is the appearance of the analog image: photography. The *animated* analog image (cinema) is an extension of this which has its own specificities, but we cannot understand them without first giving an account of the photographic event.

Another great event as regards images, specific to the twentieth century, is (along with live transmission [*la transmission en direct*], which I'm not going to discuss here) the appearance of the digital image, which is usually called the computer-generated image [*l'image de synthèse*], or calculated image: a modeling of the real that can imitate reality quasi-perfectly.

A great event specific to the end of the twentieth century, which will make itself felt, there can be no question, at the beginning of the coming century, is the appearance of the *analogico-digital image*. This image will have extreme consequences *for our intelligence of movement*.

In fact, the analogico-digital image is the beginning of a *systematic discretization of movement* – that is to say, of a vast process of the *grammaticalization of the visible*. Just as, today, the language industries are producing digital dictionaries (which is also to say, grammars), there are presently being realized "grammars" and "dictionaries" (libraries of animated objects) in the movement industries (they are industries of movement in every sense). These involve, in effect, simulations in physics, chemistry and astrophysics, simulations in training and ergonomics, virtual worlds, clones of real beings, artificial intelligence, form recognition, artificial life, and artificial death. All of this is animation.

In order to understand what is taking place with the discretization of movement, we must first analyze what the analogico-digital is, in what way it is new and why it *implies* the generalization of this discretization in the domain of animated images.

In a general way, a technical development suspends or calls into question a situation which previously seemed stable. Great moments of technical innovation are moments of suspension. In its development, the technics that interrupts one state of things imposes another. We are in such a period with regard, in particular, to images and sounds, the material supports of the bulk of our *beliefs*. Like Thomas, we believe what we see or hear: what we perceive. But today, we perceive, most of the time, through the intermediary of prostheses of perception. This means that the *conditions in which our beliefs are constituted* have entered into a phase of intense evolution.[2] Analogico-digital technology is a decisive moment in this evolution.

In Greek, suspension or interruption is *ēpokhē*: this philosophical word is the main concept of phenomenology, which Barthes mobilizes in his study of photography. Barthes himself proposes (but in a sense that subverts every classical phenomenology) that photography constitutes an *ēpokhē* in the relation to time, to memory, and to death.

Analogico-digital technology continues and amplifies a process of suspension that began a long time ago, in which the *analog* photograph was itself only a singular epoch. And so the process is ancient, but the current phase of suspension – in the form of digital photography – engenders an anxiety and a doubt which are particularly interesting, but also particularly threatening.

149

The *digital* photograph suspends a certain spontaneous belief which the analog photograph bore within itself. When I look at a digital photo, I can never be absolutely sure that what I see truly exists – nor, since it is still a question of a photo, that it does not exist at all. The analogico-digital image calls into question what André Bazin calls *the objectivity of the lens* [l'objectivité de l'objectif] in analog photography, what Barthes also calls the *this was* [*le* ça a été], the noeme of the photo. The noeme of the photo is what in phenomenology would be called its intentionality. It is what I see *always already, in advance*, in every (analog) photo: that *what is captured on the paper really was*. This is an *essential* attribute of the analog photo. That it would then be possible to manipulate this photo, to alter what was, this is another attribute, but it can only be accidental; it is not necessarily co-implied by the photo. This may happen, but it is not the rule. The rule is that every analog photo presupposes that what was photographed was (real).

Manipulation is on the contrary the essence, that is to say, the rule of the digital photo. And this possibility, which is *essential* to the digital photographic image, of *not having been*, inspires *fear* – for this image, at the same time that it is infinitely manipulable, *remains* a photo, it preserves something of the *this was* within itself, and the possibility of distinguishing the true from the false dwindles in proportion as the possibilities for the digital treatment of photos grow.

And yet, well before the digital photo existed, there were exploitations of this "accidental" potential for manipulation of the analog photo, and these exploitations have become generalized in the mass media in recent years. They have become manifest and massive, but without for all that effacing the *this was* effect. In a doctored analog photo, there is something of the *this was* (it is essential to every photo). I can never simply say: This was not. I *have to* say: *This was*, but there is *something*, however, *that isn't quite right*.

The public has suddenly become aware of this duplicity with affairs like Timisoara,[3] the fake interview with Fidel Castro,[4] or more enormous and more complex, with the role of CNN during the war in the Persian Gulf.

This is only the case because, if it is essential to the analog photo that what it shows was, it nonetheless remains the case that the analog photo is a *technical synthesis*. It is artifactual and, for this very reason, irreducibly ("essentially") exposed to its own "accidental" potential for falsification of what it presents to view. In order for this falsification to be totally effective, two things are simultaneously necessary: on the one hand, the belief that *this was*, which is objectively grounded by the technical characteristics of the photo – and I am going to come back to this – and, on the other hand, the manipulation which alters what was. If these two possibilities of the analog image did not exist *at one and the same time*, information – for example, televisual information – could not be massively doctored while at the same time preserving *intact* the effects of immediate belief, no matter how serious the crisis the media are currently going through.

But above all, even without *meaning* to doctor images, their editing, for example, engenders an essential delusion which does not however absolutely efface the *indubitable fact* that what I see was – even if it was other than *how* I see it. This manipulability inherent in analog images (as in every image-object) is further complicated by the fact that what Barthes calls the photographic reality effect [*effet de réel*] negotiates with live transmission or transmission in "real time." What is already there in all editing becomes massively problematic when it occurs live, in the temporal flow of current events [*des actualités*]. For this flow has the effect both of occulting more profoundly the artifices of imaging and of staging (by virtue of the impossibility of reversing the flow, in which "pieces of information come one after another") and of blurring the difference, by the same token, between reality and fiction – and even of making this difference impossible (to the extent that the event, covered in real time, integrates *within its very structure as event* the effects of its "coverage").

These possibilities engender a phantasmagoria that in recent years has given rise to a dangerous doubt which affects democracy, a doubt which is not very far from panic, and which is decomposing the social bond – and *to which must be opposed another doubt, another decomposition*, which is *resolute* and, as much as *possible*, conscious of itself. (But I'm not sure that this kind of consciousness is as possible as one might wish.) In effect, the analogico-digital image-object, which I shall also call the discrete image, and I shall explain this forthwith, may contribute to the emergence of new forms of "objective analysis" and of "subject-ive synthesis" of the visible – and to the emergence, by the same token, of another kind of belief and disbelief with respect to what is shown and what happens. *A more knowing belief, and by the same token, a less insipid and credulous one: this is what the things we fear about the analogico-digital photo would also make possible.*

The digitization of the analog destabilizes our knowledge of the *this was*, and we are afraid of this. But we were afraid of the analog, too: in the first photographs, we saw phantoms.

The image-object printed on photosensitive paper as *this was*, Barthes calls the *spectrum*. This specter is produced by touch – but by a type of touch that is very singular. Nadar took Baudelaire's picture, and between Baudelaire and myself there is a chain, a *contiguity of luminances*: when I look at this portrait, *I know intimately* that the luminances that come to *touch my eye* touched, that they *really* touched Baudelaire. This whole chain of duplications, from Nadar to me, is necessary in order for the photo-graphic reality *effect* to take place, this whole "umbilical cord" constituted by the photons that come to imprint and *physically* touch, from out of the nineteenth century, the *photosensitive* silver halides. A veritable photonic matter has to have been trans-mitted by having been replicated until it reached and came to touch me. If this very "real" materiality of the process engenders a *ghostly* effect, this is because Baudelaire touches me but *I* am not able to touch him. I know that I'm not going to be able to touch Baudelaire by putting my finger on his photographed face: he is dead and gone. And yet, the luminances that emanated from Baudelaire's face at the moment Nadar's camera captured and froze it forever *still touch me, beyond the shadow of a doubt.* This is moving [*é-mouvant*] (it arouses, in me, a dull movement): the ghostly effect is, in this instance, the sentiment of an absolute *irreversibility.* And this is what is so singular about this "touch": it touches me, I'm touched, but I'm not able to touch. I'm not able to be "touched" and "toucher" [*"touché-touchant"*].

What *else* are we afraid of in the analogico-digitial? We are afraid of a *night light.* Barthes too, already, spoke of a night: the night of the past that I didn't live. The light of photography comes to us from the night of a past that I didn't live, but once [*un jour*] this night was day [*cette nuit fut le jour*]. It has irreversibly become night, this is what the past is (and the phantom). But the day has to have touched the silver halides first. With analog light, the silver luminances still have to do with touch and with life – with a past life. With the digital photo, this light, from out of the night, *no longer comes entirely from the day*, it doesn't come from a past day that would simply have become night (like the photons emanating from Baudelaire's face). It comes from Hades, from the realm of the dead, from underground: it is an electric light, set free by materials from deep within the belly of the earth.[5] An *electronic*, that is to say, a *decomposed* light.

In the digital night, touch is blurred, the chain becomes complicated. It doesn't completely disappear: we're still looking at a photo. But something has intervened – treatment as binary calculation – which renders transmission uncertain. Digitization *breaks* the chain, it introduces manipulation *even into* the *spectrum*, and by the same token, *it makes phantoms and phantasms indistinct*. Photons become pixels that are in turn reduced to zeros and ones on which discrete calculations can be performed. Essentially *indubitable* when it is analog (whatever its accidental manipulability), the *this was* has become essentially *doubtful* when it is digital (it is nonmanipulation that becomes accidental).

For the imprinting of luminances on the photosensitive support – where the envelope of what is captured by the lens is laid down *immediately*, as on a retina – the analogico-digital substitutes a deferred time: the time of storage as a calculation that decomposes the *elements* of the spectrum while waiting for the treatments that will end in the imprinting of *something else*, of something *other than* the photonic ectoplasm of a *this was*.

What is new about this phantomachia, its stake, its threat, and its chance, is discretization – decomposition, the night in which, analyzed, "that which was" becomes discontinuous. *Continuity* is the condition of possibility of the Barthesian *this was*: we must have a *sense* of *continuity*, of the continuity, *not simply of the chain of luminances, but of what is seen as well*. The grain must be effaced in order for the *spectrum* to create unity, in order for it to present itself as individual (indivisible singularity, *tode ti*), as this here (*this was*) in its unique character in its unique instant, and not to appear to be treatable [*traitable*] itself as such (in order for it to produce this *punctum* that Barthes also calls, precisely, the "Intractable" [*l'"Intraitable"*]): the photographer *does not manipulate* the grain that is printed on the paper as an effect of the luminances – at least not in a discrete way. Of course, in developing, in "treatment", etc., there is a certain manipulation of the grain, a certain treatment by the photographer. The art must pass through this. However, even if the grain can be massively enlarged or diminished, one doesn't have *differentiated* access to the grains, one cannot *separate different types* of grains – except in very exceptional cases, and in a nonphotographic manner. In printing, one can play with the grain, but one does not have access to the *diacritical* manipulation of the light and of all the elements *which are differentiated therein* in order to constitute the image – which on the contrary is made possible by digitization and its "surgical precision."

This discretization radically affects the chain of memorial light, the Barthesian luminance, and by extension the *belief* we have in the image, since it was only this chain *and the intuitive knowledge we have of it* that led to this belief. Nevertheless, discretization affects it *only to a point*, and that's the interesting part. The chain of memorial light is not *absolutely* broken, it is rather knotted in a different way – otherwise, *there wouldn't even be a photograph anymore*; we wouldn't be able to speak of digital *photography*; we would say we were dealing with the computer-generated image [*l'image de synthèse*]. But there is a photograph, and it is digital, which is to say that there is day *and* night light. And by the same token, there is uncertainty about touch: did the analogico-digital luminances really touch the sensitive plate *once* [un jour]? At the same time, I know that this thing has to have touched, but I'm not sure: how much did it touch? To what *point*? Which "*punctum*" actually touches me?

No one can know if the ectoplasms which analogico-digital photos present really touched the sensitive plate once [*un jour*].

This uncertainty about touch would also be the chance of a new intelligibility of light, which has always already been at one and the same time daylight, night light, light in the night – a night still deeper even than that of a past, the night of a past that was *never present*: the weft of our dreams, of these dreams of which Prospero says we are made.

This double dimension of light and the uncertainty or *nonknowledge* that follows from it become irreducible here. It is always on the basis of the irreducibility of a nonknowledge that a knowledge is constituted.

Everything hinges here on the question of the continuity (of the memorial chain, of the *spectrum* itself) that is broken by discretization.

In extending Benjamin's analyses (which would have to be critiqued), we must distinguish the following:

- the reproducibility of the letter, first handwritten and then printed;
- analog reproducibility (i.e. photographic and cinematographic), which Benjamin studied extensively;
- digital reproducibility.

In the West, these three great types of reproducibility have constituted and overdetermined the great *epochs* of memory and the relations to time. Until now, the specificities of the different epochs of reproducibility had essentially been emphasized through a play of oppositions. In particular, with the analog on the one side, the literal and the digital on the other, it was thought that we were dealing, on the one hand, with the continuous and, on the other, with the discontinuous (or discrete).[6] It is in this sense that the image has seemed resistant to the semiological analysis inspired by Saussure, which presupposes the existence of a system of discrete elements, finite in number.

The analogico-digital technology of the image (which combines two types of reproducibility which are therefore not opposed) calls, at present, for a theoretical overcoming of these oppositions, the terms of which have in fact never ceased to *negotiate* with one another. The continuity of the analog image is a reality effect which ought not to conceal the fact that *the analog image is always already discrete*. Not simply because it is composed of atomic grains, but because it is subject to framing operations and choices about depth of field, because it has its reality effect according to the photographic and literal context in which it is inserted, etc. To say nothing of possible falsifications, it always carries a principle of the reduction of its *this was* within itself.

This can of course be seen more clearly in the animated image, in which a plurality of discontinuous images are sequentially connected, the art of the director and of the editor consisting in *effacing* this discontinuity (in occulting it) *by playing with it*. By utilizing the discontinuity of the image, they put continuity to work on the side of the *spectatorial synthesis*, which is what, for example, the *belief* that *this was* is. On the side of production and of realization, we are not engaged in synthesis: we are engaged in *analysis*. And it takes a good artist to let the spectator make the synthesis. The artist's job is to assemble the analytic elements such that the synthesis will be made more effectively. This assembling is a *logos*. The spectatorial synthesis will be made as much by the play of retinal persistence as by that of *expectations* of sequential connections (these dreams we mentioned, shared by artist and spectator alike) which efface the discontinuity of a montage all the more effectively the more cleverly it is orchestrated. These expectations, about which there would be much to say, are the phantoms and phantasms that inhabit every consciousness, which are reactivated or reanimated by the image-objects. Animation is always reanimation.

Discretization is going to go very far. Relatively basic techniques already make it possible to discretize planes, for example, in order to highlight changes in plane *which we don't see* when we watch a televised news program, which we forget, and it is only insofar as we don't see them that we look at or watch the image.[7] We must effect a change in attitude in order to be able to see them. They have an effect on us only insofar as we don't see them.

The image is always discrete, but it is always discrete, as it were, as discreetly as possible. If it were discrete indiscreetly (*shamelessly* as it were), its discreteness would have no effect on us.

The machine "sees" planes, detects them automatically, mechanically. *Because it neither believes nor knows anything, it isn't afraid of any defect, it isn't haunted by any ghosts.* And it shows, like a clock [*elle montre comme une montre*],[8] that there is a multitude of similar discontinuities in a film.

In the future, digital technology is going to go very far in spotting them: in addition to planes, it will recognize *automatically* different camera movements, identical objects present in a film, recurrent characters, voices, sets, etc. It will be possible to make indexes of these things, to inscribe them in temporal scales. This will allow us to navigate through the flow of images in a nonlinear fashion toward ever finer and more iterative elements, in the same way that we've been able to in books ever since there have been tables of contents and indexes, and what is more, it will allow us to navigate in hypertexts, which will in this way truly become hypermedia. We will be able to find all the occurrences in a film of a set, an object, a character, to analyze camera movements, identify types of planes, and in the end, every kind of discrete regularity. These techniques were first developed for the color-ization of black and white films. Combined with already existing (although still rarely used) techniques of electronic annotation, these software devices will make it possible to develop a veritable analysis of the animated image.

To this must furthermore be added synthetic libraries of objects and of movements, expressions, sounds, etc., techniques of inter-polation, of "morphing," cloning, embedding, capture, and, more generally, of the special effects elaborated by the computer-generated image industry. This is to say nothing of virtual reality, whose analogico-digital future seems assured.

Now that it has been integrated into all the techniques of simula-tion made possible by digital treatment, the photographic reality effect of which Barthes speaks may just as much be diminished as intensified: it may attain its properly *critical* stage. As a discretiza-tion of analog continuity, digitization opens the possibility of new knowledges of the image – artistic as well as theoretical and scientific.

This new cognizance [*connaissance*] stands in sharp relief against the background of the prior and intuitive knowledge I have of the analog *this was*, as well as of the analogico-digital "*perhaps this was not.*" This belief and incredulity are nothing other than the synthesis effected by the *spectator* [in English in the original], who intentionalizes the *spectrum* as having been. By discretizing the continuous, digitization allows us to submit the *this was* to a *decomposing* analysis. Essentially synthetic (for example, in the spontaneous synthesis of the *this was*), the spectator's relation to the image thus becomes an *analytic* relation as well.

*The question is therefore the relation between synthesis and analysis.*

But first, let us state precisely the *double sense* of the word "synthesis" here.

The noeme of the photograph is something that derives from the side of intention, that is to say, from the side of what philosophy calls the *synthesis* effected by the spectator, and not from the side of the *other* synthesis: the one effected *by the machine*.

We must in fact take *two* syntheses into account: one corresponds to the technical artifact in general, the other to the activity of the subject "spontaneously" producing its "mental images." However, Barthes shows perfectly well that it is the technological synthesis effected by the machine (the camera) that makes the intentional synthesis *possible*, that is to say, the *belief* in the *this was*.

And this also means that, here, to *look at* an image, as well as to synthesize it *as* a mental image, is to *know* something about the technical, synthetic, and artifactual conditions of its production – in this case, about the memorial chain in which the silver luminances are replicated.

To the three kinds of images that have appeared since the nineteenth century – analog, digital, and analogico-digital – there belong *three kinds of intuitive technical knowledges of the conditions of production of images*, to which there correspond *three different kinds of belief.*[9]

If neuropsychology rightly distinguishes the photographic image, or the image-object in general, and the visual image, and if it is clearly very important to study what happens on the side of the spectator from a neuropsychological point of view, it nonetheless remains the case that the visual image is always synthetic in both senses of the word: the spectator is affected, *in the very way* in which he synthesizes, by the photo-graphic image as receptacle of the silver effect without which the photographic noeme *would not take*. When we say that the *this was* effect, synthesis as belief, is on the side of the spectator, we are talking about a combination of two syntheses (spectator and productive camera) which engenders a ghost. This genesis presupposes this duality, for which psychology will never be enough: it requires technology, without which there is no image-object, nor by extension any mental image. (But phenomenology *in the strict sense*, which Barthes calls into question by emphasizing the *technical* conditions of synthesis, is not enough either.) Consequently, the synthesis of the "subject" stems from the knowledge he has of the technical conditions of the image-object's production, insofar as this object is also a trace, a souvenir-object overdetermining a relation to time (a way that the past has of giving itself to the present). The spirituality of psychology (as well as of phenomenology), of what is on the side of the visual image, is always affected by the essentially ghostly, phantasmatic, and artificial spirituality of technology as well. Every visual image, whether that of *Homo sapiens sapiens*, of Lascaux, of the pictorial image properly speaking, that of the analog photographic image or of the analogico-digital image, is always already affected by the *spirituality of the technology it looks at* – from the vantage of a certain knowledge which it has of this technology. The visual image articulated on the objectivity of the lens [*sur l'objectivité de l'objectif*] knows that *this was*. It knows or it thinks it knows, and it is to precisely this extent that the nervous system studied by the neuropsychologist can reconstruct the real: according to the requirements of a *possible technology which it knows*. The nervous system knows what is possible, and it is on the basis of the knowledge it has of what is possible that it "realizes" what it sees.

When the visual image knows that, from now on, photography can represent what has never materialized before the lens, it begins not to look at the photographic image of the *this was* in the same way anymore. Called into question before every image, whether analog or analogico-digital, the visual image plunges into a new form of knowledge because it knows that within its knowledge is inscribed an irreducible nonknowledge of the image.[10]

The analogico-digital technology of images (just like that of sounds) opens the epoch of the analytic apprehension of the image-object. And because synthesis is double, the gain in new analytic capacities is also a gain in new synthetic capacities. Because this discretization concerns everything that had previously been grasped as constituting a continuity, the gaze that "intentionalizes" every frame necessarily ends up progressively transformed.

To a point, this transformation is comparable to what occurs when, in the seventh century BCE, in ancient Greece, the discretization of speech is brought about by the generalization of alphabetic writing. Speech, too, would engender effects of continuity which are largely transformed, in their conditions of analysis and of synthesis, with the appearance of writing. In a so-called society without writing, the speaker has a relation of continuity to his own speech and to the speech of the other. In this speech, he hears no discrete elements. We, the literate, *believe we know* that there is, in all speech, a play of analyzable, diacritical combinatorial elements, which form a sign system, but the "spontaneous" attitude, especially in a society in which there is no writing in the everyday sense, is to perceive this as a whole. As a continuity. This is the same relation that we have had until now to the animated photographic image.

The Western relation to language, which must *pass* through analysis (through schooling), synthesizes in a different way: we have been living, since Greece, in the critical era of the relation to language that gave rise to logic, philosophy, science, etc. – as well as to great historical and political crises. What happens first with the analog and, now, with the analogico-digital is of the same order. There is a great crisis, a generalized questioning, comparable to what had taken place in Greece with respect to language (of which sophistry and the philosophical response to it are epistemic consequences). From this crisis was born a critique, an extremely dynamic power of analysis, which both troubled the historical present by exposing it to the night of its past, which had literally been preserved, and brought to it lucidity, a new kind of light, an *Aufklärung*, so to speak. We ought not to forget that this epoch was also afraid of writing. Writing, whose science is grammar.

Grammar is normative: it is not an apodictic (ideal and noncontradictory) science. A grammar, in the everyday sense of the word, describes a language state which it selects from among other language states. We have known at least since Saussure that "a" language is an artificial thing: a language is always already languages. Every idiom is determined, at every level of speech, in a dialectical and idiolectical way. In other words, when a grammarian describes the rules of "the" language, in reality he describes the rules according to which he speaks his own language, his own idiolect, which is only one instance of a diachronic, evolving, and localized system. What the grammarian does is consecrate one usage, which he calls "good usage." No grammatical operation is ever pure. And when one talks about deep, universal structures, as in Chomsky, then one is not talking about the grammar of a language, but about universal rules governing linguistic competence prior to any real language – which I doubt exist and which I doubt are rules (they are rather an originary irregularity: a *lack* of rule, a *law of exception* – I am not able to develop this point here). This means that there are never pure rules of *competence* which would precede those rules brought into play and *invented* in the course of *performances*.

As for movement and for what happens to movement with the analogico-digital image, the consequences are as follows: if it is true that the animated analogico-digital necessarily brings new rules of movement to light, the *description* of this movement is its transformation. That is to say, it is not only its description, but rather its *inscription*: its *invention*.

The grammatical operator is, above all, technology itself: the discretization of the "continuity" of the image-object is going to be carried out in relation to technoscientific opportunity (the discovery of this or that algorithm of form recognition, for example), and not on the basis of a decision made by a "grammarian." This or that algorithm is developed in relation to industrial strategies and battles for norms which are already underway. Here, it is important that the artistic and intellectual community know how to seize opportunities and take part in the choices that will be made in orienting research and development.

The analysis I've proposed, of the two syntheses (spectator and camera), such as they can never be separated from each other, signifies that the *evolution of the technical synthesis* implies the *evolution of the spectatorial synthesis*. Both syntheses are actually constituted in the course of what Simondon called a transductive relation (a relation which constitutes its terms, in which one term cannot precede the other because they exist only in the relation). That is to say, new image-objects are going to engender new mental images, as well as another intelligence of movement, for it is essentially a question of animated images. The intelligence I'm talking about here is not the intelligence of what I called the new knowledges of the image. It designates techno-intuitive knowledges – intentions in the Barthesian sense – of a new kind, which will of course be, moreover, affected or able to be affected by new knowledges, and that's the *opportunity* [la chance].

I placed myself, at the beginning of my study, under the authority of the critique proposed by Derrida, twenty-five years ago, of the opposition of the signifier and the signified. You no doubt know that one major result of this critique is that language is always already writing, and that, contrary to appearances, we should not suppose that there is first an oral language and then a written copy of this language, but that, in order for language to be written in the everyday sense, it must *already* be a writing: a system of traces, of "grammē," of discrete elements. I will say, in conclusion, while getting rather far ahead of myself and in a purely programmatic way, that we must posit the following hypothesis: life (*anima* – on the side of the mental image) is always *already* cinema (animation – image-object). The technological synthesis is not a replica, not a double of life, any more than writing is a replication of speech, but there is a complex of writing in which the two terms always move together, being in transductive relation. Obviously, we would have to do a whole history of representation from this point of view. A history that would be, first of all, the history of the material supports of image-objects. And we would have to mark the specificity of certain epochs: just as certain kinds of writing actually liberate certain kinds of reflexivity (for example, certain kinds of linear, alphabetic writing, without which law, science, and in particular history would be inconceivable), so certain kinds of image-objects are doubtless destined to liberate *reflexivity* in the domains of the visible and of movement, just as alphabetic writing reveals the discrete characters of language.

Techniques for the digitization of animated images are going to become very widespread in global society through multimedia and digital television. The relation to the analog image is going to be massively discretized, thrown into crisis, it is going to open up a critical access to the image. There is a chance, if it can be seized, to develop a culture of *reception*. Which might lead to another way of formulating the question of the cultural exception. The real problem here is to rethink or think otherwise what Hollywood has up to this point done in the domain of the culture industry, to which cinema and television belong. For what it has done, it has done in accordance with a *reifying schema, and by opposing production to consumption, that is to say: by putting analysis on one side (production) and synthesis on the other (consumption)*. Technology is giving us the chance to modify this relation, in a direction that would bring it closer to the relation of the literate person to literature: it is not possible to synthesize a book without having analyzed literally oneself. It is not possible to read without knowing how to write. And soon it will be possible to see an image analytically: "television" ["*l'écran*"] and "text" ["*l'écrit*"] are not simply opposed.

# NOTES

## Artifactualities
### Jacques Derrida

1  The expression here, *espace public*, might also be translated as "public sphere." (Trans.)

2  The French *actualité* is, for the purposes of this text, strictly untranslatable. In the singular and at its most abstract, *actualité* means something like "topicality" or "relevance," but with a decidedly temporal emphasis. More concretely, *l'actualité* is what is topical or relevant at a given moment, this moment being generally understood as "our moment," or "now." Thus what is *actuel* is what is currently (or *actuellement*) happening – what one might be tempted to translate as "present" or "present-day" if Derrida did not distinguish *actualité*, precisely, from the present, below. *Actuel* can also mean something quite close to the English "actual," in the sense of what is "acting" or "enacted" – what is "in effect" as opposed to potential or virtual. But again, it is precisely this opposition that Derrida calls into question here. In the plural, *les actualités* means something like "current events," or even, quite simply, "the news."

I give "actuality" for *actualité* in hopes that at least some of the work that the word is made to do will remain at least minimally legible. Other forms I translate variously, inserting the French in brackets in the text of "Artifactualities" only. (Trans.)

3  In this and following sentences, Derrida plays on the relationships among a series of words, the most important of which – between "fact" or "factuality" and *faire* ("to make or do") – is untranslatable in English. (Trans.)

4  The expression here is *se rendre à*, which can mean both "to surrender" and "to go to" or "head toward" something. (Trans.)

164

5   Lost in English here is the play on the dimensions of the television screen, *l'écran de la plus grande exposition*, and those of the "superstore" – *grande surface* (literally, "large surface"). (Trans.)

6   The *droit de réponse* states that anyone accused of wrongdoing in a newspaper article has the right to a published response in the same paper. The law was extended to radio and television on April 6, 1987. (Trans.)

7   *La justesse*: "justness," in the sense, now obsolete in English, of accuracy, correctness or conformity to a norm. (Trans.)

8   The French word here, *férance*, is not in fact a word but a fragment of a word that calls our attention to the Latin roots of *différance*: *dis-*, apart + *ferre*, to carry. Thus "ference" can be read as the carrying-back or "report" of a rapport or relation (of a re-ference), or as a variation on the "ferral" of "deferral" (the French verb *différer* means both "to differ" and "to defer"). (Trans.)

9   In this and the following sentence, the expression is *se rendre à*. See note 4 on its double meaning, above. (Trans.)

10  *Force de loi. Le "fondement mystique de l'autorité"* (Paris: Galilée, 1994); see, in English, "Force of Law: The 'Mystical Foundation of Authority'," trans. Mary Quaintance, in *Deconstruction and the Possibility of Justice*, ed. Drucilla Cornell, Michel Rosenfeld, David Gray Carlson (New York: Routledge, 1992). *Spectres de Marx* (Paris: Galilée, 1993); see, in English, *Specters of Marx*, trans. Peggy Kamuf (New York: Routledge, 1994).

11  The sentence makes little sense in English, in which both *la venue* and *le venir* must be translated as "coming." Indeed, it should be noted that in this and following sentences Derrida brings an entire constellation of nouns derived from the verbs *venir* (to come) and *arriver* (to arrive, come, or happen) into play. Whereas the afore-mentioned *venue* can include senses of coming as diverse as the coming of "comings and goings" and the advent of Christ, *l'arrivée* seems to denote only those comings for which there is a horizon of expectation (such as those of a train or plane, or of the friend with whom we have a date). Derrida, however, introduces a third term: *l'arrivance*. I give "coming" for *venue*, and "arrival" for both *arrivée* and *arrivance*, inserting, in the latter case, the French in brackets in the text. Finally, there is *l'arrivant*, which in everyday usage means "one who comes" or "one who is arriving," as in the "newcomer" or "new arrival." Following the English translations of both *Specters of Marx* and *Aporias* (trans. Thomas Dutoit (Stanford: Stanford University Press, 1993)), I leave *arrivant* untranslated throughout. For Derrida's own account of the word, see *Aporias*, pp. 33–5. The reader should at

the very least keep in mind that the *arrivant* and the "absolute" or "messianic" arrival (*l'arrivance*) correspond, and that their mutual relation to what happens (*ce qui arrive*), or the event, although unmistakable in French, is untranslatable in English. It should also be noted that what I almost invariably give as "the event," *l'événement*, might also (and, sometimes, better) be translated as "happening." (Trans.)

12   The word for "ghost" here, *revenant*, means, literally, "one who comes back," allowing for a wordplay that is lost in English. I give *revenant* in brackets throughout this volume in order to distinguish it from *fantôme*, for which I give sometimes "phantom," sometimes "ghost." On the distinctions Derrida makes among the three French words, *revenant*, *fantôme*, and *spectre*, see "Spectrographies," chapter 8 below. (Trans.)

13   While I translate *enfant*, as it is ordinarily translated in English, as "child," there is a suggestion that we are to hear the Latin root here: *infans*: *in–* , the negative or privative prefix and *fans*, present participle of *fari*, to speak. The "infant" cannot speak. (Trans.)

14   *Apories. Mourir – s'attendre aux "limites de la vérité"* (Paris: Galilée, 1996) (originally published in *Le Passage des frontières. Autour du travail de Jacques Derrida* (Paris: Galilée, 1993)); see, in English, *Aporias*, in note 11 above.

15   Jean-Marie Le Pen: founder (1972) and leader of the Front National (National Front), an extreme-right party in France. Among the elements of the party platform are increased state protection of domestic industry, drastic reform of laws pertaining to immigration and naturalization (ban and expulsion of non-European immigrants) and, correlative to these objectives, tightened European border controls. (Trans.)

16   Charles Pasqua: French politician and Minister of the Interior, 1986–8 and 1993–5. The "Pasqua Law," the stated aim of which was to curb illegal immigration by further restricting the entry of foreign nationals, was passed in August 1986, then revoked in May 1989, on the grounds that several of its articles (on the prolonged detention of foreigners) were unconstitutional. (Trans.)

17   The *sécuritaires* are, as their name suggests, those who are security conscious (or, some would say, obsessed). The name also suggests a pun on *sanitaires*, a common euphemism for the WC or toilet. (Trans.)

18   Particularly in *Donner le temps, I. La fausse monnaie* (Paris: Galilée, 1992); see, in English, *Given Time, I. Counterfeit Money*, trans. Peggy Kamuf (Chicago: University of Chicago Press, 1992); and in "Force of Law," in note 10 above.

19  Emmanuel Levinas, *Totalité et infini* (The Hague: Martinus Nijhoff, 1961), p. 62; see, in English, *Totality and Infinity*, trans. Alphonso Lingis (Pittsburgh: Duquesne University Press, 1969), p. 89.
20  The "Vélodrome d'Hiver," or "Vel d'Hiv," has come to refer, metonymically, to the arrest and detainment by French authorities of 13,000 Parisian Jews on July 16–17, 1942. The majority were held in the velodrome in atrocious conditions before being deported to Auschwitz. (Trans.)

# Echographies of Television
## *Jacques Derrida and Bernard Stiegler*

### 1  Right of Inspection

1  In the literal sense: the interview was filmed in Derrida's home. (Trans.)
2  Jacques Derrida, *Lecture de "Droit de regard" de Marie-Françoise Plissart* (Paris: Minuit, 1982); see, in English, *Right of Inspection*, trans. David Wills (New York: Monacelli Press, 1998).
3  The *dépôt légal* is the practice, required by French law, of depositing a copy or copies of every publication with state authorities to be included in the national archives or collections. (Trans.)
4  At the time this interview was recorded, the decree had not yet been issued. It was published in the *Journal officiel* on January 1, 1994.
5  It should be noted that in this and following paragraphs Derrida plays on the expression, "live television," or *la télévision en direct*, in both French and English. I have not been consistent in my translation of *en direct*, giving sometimes "live," sometimes "direct," according to context. I have indicated those places where the word "live" appears in English in the original in brackets in the text. (Trans.)

### 2  Artifactuality, Homohegemony

1  "Artifactualities," partially reproduced above.
2  In French, one refers to "the ratings," metonymically, as the *Audimat*, or "automatic Audimeter," a machine for the automatic measurement (via telephone networks) of television audiences. (Trans.)
3  The expression *exception culturelle* is a kind of shorthand for the exclusion (or "exception") of the French film and television industries from global trade negotiations on deregulation on the grounds of preserving cultural and linguistic integrity. (Trans.)

4  Four-year-old Grégory Villemin was found dead in the Vologne river in the department of Vosges on October 16, 1984. Within months, the child's father had murdered his (the father's) cousin, accused by his sister-in-law (who later retracted) of having murdered the child. There followed a series of trials which garnered extraordinary media attention and which in fact continue to do so at the time of this translation. (Trans.)

5  The word here is *instruction*: a preliminary phase of the French judicial process in which a magistrate attempts to assess the merits of a case. (Trans.)

6  On this "who" and "what," see Bernard Stiegler, *La technique et le temps*, vol.1, *La faute d'Épiméthée* (Paris: Galilée, 1994), and vol. 2, *La désorientation* (Paris: Galilée, 1996); for an English translation of volume 1, see *Technics and Time*, trans. Richard Beardsworth and George Collins (Stanford: Stanford University Press, 1998).

7  In fact, Patrick Poivre d'Arvor never had an interview with Castro. He used images produced during a press conference in order to simulate an interview which he then tried to pass off as a "scoop."

8  His lawyer would above all claim that the TV Carton Jaune association was not qualified to represent the collective body of television viewers and that, as a restricted group, representing only itself, it could not be party to a civil suit on charges of damages resulting from the program in question. All of which raises enormous legal questions with respect to the current status of the journalist's profession. To whom is the journalist legally responsible if he is beyond the "professional" judgment of collective authorities [*des instances corporatives*]?

9  André Leroi-Gourhan, *Le geste et la parole* (Paris: Albin Michel, 1964–5); see, in English, *Gesture and Speech*, trans. Anna Bostock Berger (Cambridge: MIT Press, 1993).

## 3  Acts of Memory: Topolitics and Teletechnology

1  The French word here is *la technique*, for which I sometimes give "technique" and, sometimes, "technics." The distinction does not exist in French, and in English we are left with a choice between a word that is often too specific or concrete ("technique," in the sense of a skill or procedure) and a word that is often too general ("technics," which denotes at once a collection of such skills, procedures, or ways of doing and something more elusive and essential – what we might think of as "technology" but minus, precisely, the implication of the scientific or the rational). The reader should keep in mind that, for the purposes of this text, both senses are operative throughout. (Trans.)

2 Jules Ferry: prime minister of France, 1880–1, 1883–5. Ferry was especially active in the reform of public education, holding that the "education of the people" would guarantee the future of democracy. Perhaps not coincidentally, he is also remembered for his expansion of France's colonial empire. (Trans.)

3 On this argument or hypothesis, see Jacques Derrida, "Foi et savoir. Les deux sources de la religion aux limites de la raison," in *La religion*, ed. Jacques Derrida and Gianni Vattimo (Paris: Seuil, 1996); see, in English, "Faith and Knowledge: The Two Sources of 'Religion' at the Limits of Mere Reason," trans. Samuel Weber, in *Religion*, ed. Jacques Derrida and Gianni Vattimo (Stanford: Stanford University Press, 1998).

4 The French word here is *héritage*, for which I sometimes give "heritage," sometimes "inheritance." The distinction does not exist in French, and the reader should keep in mind that, for the purposes of this text, the word can (and, in fact, always does) mean both. (Trans.)

## 4 Inheritances – and Rhythm

1 On the translation of *héritage*, see note 4 to "Acts of Memory," chapter 3 above. (Trans.)

## 5 The "Cultural Exception": the States of the State, the Event

1 In French, one ordinarily capitalizes the word "state" when referring to a government or sovereign political entity, but not when referring to a condition or mode of being (a "state of being," "state of things," etc.). Thus it is possible to play on a "statics" of the political state in a way that is not rigorously translatable in English. (Trans.)

2 On the "cultural exception," see note 3 to "Artifactuality, Homo-hegemony," chapter 2 above. (Trans.)

3 This has indeed turned out to be the case, insofar as, since the time of this interview, GATT has been subsumed by the WTO (World Trade Organization). (Trans.)

4 Jean Baudrillard, *La guerre du Golfe n'a pas eu lieu* (Paris: Galilée, 1991); see, in English, *The Gulf War Did Not Take Place*, trans. Paul Patton (Bloomington: Indiana University Press, 1995).

## 6 The Archive Market: Truth, Testimony, Evidence

1 The French *chance* is much richer semantically than its English counterpart. To say that something constitutes the market's "chance" may

be to say that it constitutes its chance or hope in the sense of its condition of possibility. In this sense it is indissociable both from risk and from promise. It may also be to say that it constitutes the happy or fortunate thing *of the market* (double genitive) – either that this thing *is* what is happy or fortunate *about the market*, or that the market is *itself* an opportunity, and thus a happy or fortunate thing. (Trans.)

2    On the translation of *la technique*, see note 1 to "Acts of Memory," chapter 3 above. (Trans.)

3    See Pierre Nora, "Le retour de l'événement," in Jacques le Goff and Pierre Nora (eds), *Faire l'histoire* (Paris: Gallimard, 1974).

4    It should be noted that the most common and everyday meaning of *échographie* is "ultrasound," and that the analogy between the (diagnostic and other) possibilities opened by medical imaging technologies and those opened by television can be understood to frame Derrida and Stiegler's entire conversation. (Trans.)

5    Roland Barthes, *La chambre claire. Note sur la photographie* (Paris: Cahiers du Cinéma, Gallimard, Seuil, 1980); see, in English, *Camera Lucida: Reflections on Photography*, trans. Richard Howard (New York: Hill and Wang, 1981). [I give page references to the English edition but, in the interest of consistency, provide my own translations throughout. (Trans.)]

## 7    Phonographies: Meaning – from Heritage to Horizon

1    On this point, see "L'époque orthographique," in Bernard Stiegler, *La désorientation*, vol. 2 of *La technique et le temps* (Paris: Galilée, 1994–6).

2    Jacques Derrida, *Mémoires. Pour Paul de Man* (Paris: Galilée, 1988); see, in English, *Mémoires: For Paul de Man* (New York: Columbia University Press, 1986).

3    See Bernard Stiegler, *La faute d'Épiméthée* (vol. 1 of *La technique et le temps*), in English as *Technics and Time*, trans. Richard Beardsworth and George Collins (Stanford: Stanford University Press, 1998).

## 8    Spectrographies

1    *Ghostdance*, dir. Ken McMullen, perf. Pascale Ogier and Jacques Derrida, Loose Yard LTD, Channel Four, ZDF, 1983.

2    See Roland Barthes, *La chambre claire. Note sur la photographie* (Paris: Cahiers du Cinéma, Gallimard, Seuil, 1980), pp. 120, 126–

7, or *Camera Lucida: Reflections on Photography*, trans. Richard Howard (New York: Hill and Wang, 1981), pp. 76, 80–1.

3  Jacques Derrida, "Les morts de Roland Barthes," in *Psyché, Inventions de l'autre* (Paris: Galilée, 1987), p. 291; see, in English, "The Deaths of Roland Barthes," trans. Pascale-Anne Brault and Michael Naas, in Hugh J. Silverman (ed.), *Philosophy and Non-Philosophy since Merleau-Ponty* (Evanston, Ill.: Northwestern University Press, 1997), pp. 259–96.

4  A commentary on this commentary can be found in the first chapter of Bernard Stiegler, *La désorientation* (Paris: Galilée, 1996).

5  The verb *regarder* may mean either "to look at" or "watch" or "to regard," in the sense of "to concern" (as in "This does not concern you," etc.). In this and following sentences, I have (rather violently) expanded the original phrases in order to give both meanings. (Trans.)

6  Lost in English here is an extended play on the prepositions *avant* and *devant*, both of which mean "before" (*avant* generally in the temporal sense, *devant* generally in the spatial), as well as on the latter's homonym, the present participle of the verb *devoir*, "to owe." Again, I have expanded what in the original is a single word or phrase into multiple phrases in English. (Trans.)

7  Martin Heidegger, *Sein und Zeit*, 17th edn (Tübingen: Max Niemeyer, 1993), p. 20; see, in English, *Being and Time*, trans. John Macquarrie and Edward Robinson (New York: Harper, 1962), p. 41. I have modified Macquarrie and Robinson's translation to follow Stiegler's French. (Trans.)

8  See *Apories: Mourir – s'attendre aux "limites de la vérité"* (Paris: Galilée, 1996), p. 110, note 1. [This note does not appear in the English edition, which was published prior to the French. (Trans.)]

9  *Unterwegs zur Sprache* (Pfullingen: Günther Neske, 1959); see, in English, *On the Way to Language*, trans. Peter D. Hertz (New York: Harper and Row, 1971).

10  Or, in the more cynical reading: "this gesture in which one thinks one is thinking the ontological difference." (Trans.)


9   Vigilances of the Unconscious


1  The Arte channel is a joint venture of France and Germany which produces and shows educational and cultural programming in both French and German. (Trans.)


171

# The Discrete Image
## Bernard Stiegler

1 Tahar Ben Jelloun wrote, after the attempted assassination of the Egyptian novelist Naguib Mahfouz (in *Le Monde*, October 19, 1994): "... there is, in his work, an utterly natural preoccupation with his people. The characters in most of his novels are people from his neighborhood.... He's their magician, the guide who keeps them company, who takes their hand.... Sticking a knife in the back of an 83-year-old man, a man who did more for Egypt than any political party, who did the country more good than any cultural attaché or tourist bureau, is like setting fire to a museum or to a great library. Only no museum, no library is worth as much as the life of a man."

2 I don't mean to suggest that, before, there would have been a perception pure of all prostheticity – quite the contrary: to say that there is no mental image without an image-object is to say that all perception is affected by technics. I mean to say that, today, prostheticity is becoming patent, and that, changing in nature, it is throwing our perception into crisis.

3 The role of television in the 1989 Romanian "revolution" remains the object of intense scrutiny and debate. Among the most critical and contested events was the televising of an apparent massacre of antigovernment demonstrators by former communist dictator Nicolae Ceausescu's security forces in Timisoara, on December 16, 1989, in which it was initially reported that 40,000 to 60,000 people had been killed. Considerable evidence emerged, after the fact, suggesting that this and other massacres had been carefully staged, and, in some cases, simply invented, and that the so-called revolution was not a popular uprising but a coup. Especially significant in this regard was the discovery that bodies of alleged massacre victims exhibited for the media were in fact corpses that had been interred long ago, under other circumstances, and disinterred for the occasion. Also televised were the dramatic flight of Ceausescu and his wife, by helicopter, from an ostensibly progovernment rally in Bucharest that had erupted in further violence, during which the national television studios were themselves attacked, and their summary "trial" and execution, on Christmas Day. (Trans.)

4 On the fake interview with Castro, see "Artifactuality, Homohegemony," chapter 2 of *Echographies*, above. (Trans.)

5   Carbon, petroleum, uranium. What Paul Virilio calls a *false day* [*un faux-jour*]. I think this light, from out of this night, comes from a night which stands at the heart of day, which is not its opposite. Unlike Virilio, I don't believe that false day is what makes us go out of day, I don't believe that night is what makes us leave the day behind. I believe that, as Heraclitus said, night is the truth of day, and day, the truth of night.

6   Benjamin does not make this kind of distinction. On the contrary, he develops the points that literal and analog reproductions have in common. He even emphasizes, with respect to film, the implementation of an analytic process from which he draws new apperceptive possibilities – that is to say, new possibilities for discretization.

7   This is the technique utilized by the Videoscribe software developed by the INA and installed on the audiovisual reading stations available to researchers through the Inathèque of France. You will find an illustration, in which the software is being used to analyze a television news program, above (opposite p. 79).

8   The computer is a clock – a machine for marking time.

9   Still one more kind would have to be added here: that of the analog image transmitted live. François Jost, in *Un monde à notre image. Énonciation, cinéma, télévision* (Paris: Méridiens/Klincksieck, 1992), has rightly pointed out that when I watch a sequence of televised images which I know is a live retransmission, I don't watch it *in the same way* as I do when the sequence has been prerecorded [*transmise en différé*]. The transmission of the image-object and the knowledge I have of it are constitutive of its effect – they condition what Jost calls the spectatorial attitude.

10  This whole process belongs to the history of the filling of a lack: a process which has been totally consubstantial with our history as humans, for 4 million years. What, as regards the filling of the lack, has changed or is changing over the course of this history and in particular today? This immense history is at one and the same time, indissolubly, that of humanity and that of technics: the history of an original lack or lack of origin [*d'un défaut d'origine*]. This original lack or lack of origin, which we never stop filling with prostheses which do nothing but intensify it in proportion as we fill it (this can be seen very clearly in analogico-digital imagery), haunts us. It haunts us like a ghost: it is the ghost or phantom. The phantoms I'm talking about here, whether that of the photograph as *this was*, of new forms of photography, of the phantoms found in computer-generated or so-called "synthetic" digital images, and

in every form of representation, which is always ghostly, all these phantoms are nothing but figures, representations (in the theatrical sense, and not in the modern philosophical or psychological senses) – Nietzsche would have said masks – of this necessary lack [*de ce défaut qu'il faut*]. This lack is necessary, for it is what drives all this machinery that we develop and that keeps us alive; it makes us want, desire, fear, love, etc. This lack is a lack of memory. Barthes understood this very well: that the photo fills a certain lack of memory by giving me access to a *this was* which I haven't lived and which nonetheless presents itself to me, bringing into play a totally phantomatic relation between presence and absence. This lack of memory I call – following Derrida, who owes the expression to the ghost of Husserl – retentional finitude. The question of analogico-digital photography is therefore nothing but a singular case of a situation that we can already analyze in the relation between the cerebral cortex and sharpened flint, between Australopithecus and Neanderthal man: we are dealing with the ghostly from the moment that man begins to cut into matter or material. From the moment that he begins to inscribe forms upon it. Photonic – including digital – material is nothing but a particular case of this "appallingly ancient" labor (I have developed this perspective in *La technique et le temps*, vol. 1, *La faute d'Épiméthée* (Paris: Galilée, 1994); or in English, *Technics and Time*, trans. Richard Beardsworth and George Collins (Stanford: Stanford University Press, 1998).